—— *A* ——

WITNESS *to*

Christ

The Testimony of a Born-Again Catholic

REVISED EDITION

by William R. Odell

Revised Edition 2020
Published by William Odell
Ellensburg, WA
Library of Congress Control Number: 2011960343
ISBN: 978-0-578-69927-1

Contents

Prologue

Father Dennis Robb, the pastor at Immaculate Conception Catholic Church in Everett, Washington, spoke in his homily of the unique promise contained in the Christian faith, a promise unlike that found in any other religion. This Christian faith offered eternal life to each of us, Father Dennis proclaimed. Not just an eternal existence for the soul, but a resurrection of the body—an eternal life spent with God and with each other in a heavenly home; freed from the bondage of sin and suffering, living in a place of breathtaking beauty and in a state of eternal peace, indescribable happiness, and all-embracing love. The concept was staggering. How incredible it would be, I thought, if one really *knew* there was a God—a loving, faithful, all-powerful Creator—not just believed it (in the sense that I understood the word "believe"), but actually *knew* it. What if one really *knew* that he would be resurrected after death? What if one really *knew* that he was destined for heaven? What if one really *knew* this life was created for a purpose—a purpose not just for our short time on this earth, but a purpose that extended through all eternity? The concept was indeed staggering. The contrast between the enormity of this Christian promise and the comparatively puny promises of other world religions was striking. I tried to imagine how I would feel, what I would do, if I believed this promise. Surely I wouldn't be able to contain myself. Maybe I'd jump up and down and shout, "Hallelujah!" I didn't know. How did Christians express their joy?

I looked around the church at the hundreds of Catholics who filled the pews that Sunday morning. Incredibly, they appeared unmoved by the pastor's message! I could not detect any outward sign of enthusiasm. No one jumped for joy. Not one "Amen" or "Hallelujah" escaped from their lips. How could they contain themselves, I wondered? How could they be reminded of this awesome, indescribably vast promise of their faith and not dance in the aisles with unbounded joy? Then a numbing thought struck me. Maybe they didn't actually believe it! Maybe they came to church every Sunday, went through all the motions, but they didn't actually believe it! That seemed unlikely, yet how else could they remain so calm?

Perhaps for some, I reflected, the message had never really reached home. Maybe they hoped, but weren't really sure it was true. Maybe others were just uncomfortable with public displays of emotion. Perhaps many more had just believed so long that they'd grown complacent with the enormity of the promise—they just couldn't imagine what it felt like not to know God or to believe in His promise. They had no "bad news" with which to contrast the "good news." They couldn't put themselves in my shoes.

Even my wife, Pam, who had somehow talked me into joining her at church that morning, didn't really believe me when I told her I didn't believe in God. She assumed I was just being dramatic. But I truly *didn't* believe in God, nor could I understand how anyone else could. To me the Christian message seemed absurd: a Messiah, sent to earth by a Supreme Being to die as atonement for the sins of all mankind, "saving" us from the eternal punishment due us for our rejection of God and our horrid and sinful treatment of one another. The Christian message seemed to me as irrational and unbelievable as Greek mythology. Regardless of the blissful imagery painted in Father Dennis' sermon, I had no intention of ever becoming a Christian.

"For the message of the cross is foolishness to those who are perishing, but to us who are being saved it is the power of God."

1 CORINTHIANS 1:18

Chapter One

The Seeds of Faith

I was in my early forties that Sunday morning when I sat in Immaculate Conception Catholic Church with my wife Pam, and my young daughter Sarah, listening to Father Dennis Robb preach about the great promise of Christianity. I don't recall how Pam talked me into going to church that day. She is a "cradle" Catholic, raised from infancy in an Irish-Catholic neighborhood in the Northeast. She never misses Sunday Mass or a Holy Day of Obligation. I, on the other hand, was raised in the Pacific Northwest in a family that, while honest and moral, was decidedly unchurched. Although my mother was a closet Christian, my father so opposed religion that Christianity was not allowed to be discussed openly in our home, and it rarely was, and never when he was in the house. In fact, I didn't even learn until decades later that I had actually been baptized as an infant in the Methodist church that my grandfather attended.

However, when I was very young, I remember my mother talking to us kids about the Bible, but not in front of Dad. She even gave each of us our own Bible. I had kept mine for many years and occasionally read from it out of curiosity. I also recall as a very young child attending a small church with my cousins a couple of times when our grandfather took us to visit them on their farm. But that was the extent of my Christian formation, and it didn't take. I didn't believe in God, most certainly not the Christian concept of God. After marrying Pam I attended Mass on Christmas and Easter, but only because she really wanted me to. It was rare to find me in church any other Sunday.

As a young man I had been a bona fide, unapologetic atheist, as I assumed my father was. To my young eyes the world appeared to be one long train wreck. Our country was embroiled in the Vietnam War. Every night the television brought us body counts and pictures of bagged American corpses being loaded onto helicopters. Angry anti-war protestors marched in the streets and burned college campus buildings. White people abused and discriminated against black people. In anger and frustration, black people rioted and looted and burned their own neighborhoods. The news from the rest of world was as bad or worse—famines, violence, genocide, and wide-spread oppression. How anyone could believe that some loving, all-powerful God had created us to be his children and then stood idly aside while we destroyed each other was beyond me. Besides, it seemed to me that science offered more plausible theories for our existence than did religion. In my kinder moments I thought Christians were naïve and gullible. In my less charitable moments, I sometimes wondered if they weren't swimming in the shallow end of the gene pool.

But as I reached my mid-twenties I began to see beyond the chaos of the human condition, and to recognize the complexity, and yes, even the miracle of creation. All life was amazingly complex, and the human being most of all. Could all of this really have come about as a result of some "big bang", the universe and its hundred-plus essential elements magically coming into being from an eternal nothing? Then these inert, lifeless elements somehow arranging themselves in simple forms that mysteriously came alive, eventually "evolving" into elephants, hummingbirds, and rose bushes? Could all creation and life really be that random? Surely there existed the possibility of some creative intelligence behind this order, some powerful intelligence behind the complexity of life itself. No, I would never believe in this myth called Christianity. However, maybe one of the other world religions presented a more accurate representation of this creative force. So I took some philosophy courses in college. I looked at eastern religions. I read the *Bhagavad-Gita*, the *Koran*, the *Autobiography of a Yogi*, and such pop culture musings as *Zen and the Art of Motorcycle Maintenance*. I learned Transcendental Meditation. Occasionally I even read from that Bible I had received as a child. My experience didn't convince me that any eastern religion contained the whole truth, although some seemed to me more plausible than Christianity. But the reading and experiences transformed me from an atheist into an agnostic. Not yet knowing the Truth, I at least suspected the Truth existed, and that it possibly centered on some form or source of creative intelligence. I even sensed that some day I might come to fully recognize who or what that intelligence was.

Then, at 30 years of age, I met my future (and present) wife—this Irish-Catholic girl with a dazzling smile and a disarming Boston accent. I fell in love. A year later we decided to marry. Pam wanted to marry in the Catholic Church. Because it was clearly important to her, I agreed. We were required to interview for the privilege. The priest asked to what faith I belonged. Having enough sense not to rock the boat, and knowing my mother was raised a Methodist (and not knowing at the time that my father had been baptized a Catholic) I told him I was a Methodist. That apparently was good enough for him. I went through a short instruction in the Catholic faith which, as I recall, mainly taught me when to sit, stand, or kneel during Mass. I also was required to promise to raise our children in the Catholic Church. I agreed, and I took this commitment seriously. I would not deny my children the experience of a Christian upbringing, even though I myself did not believe in Christianity. If I ever later discovered the real Truth, I could share it with them at that time.

Looking back, I marvel at the fortune of that decision. I've since noticed that God honors obedience. But back then I did not believe in God, nor know of His ways, nor see His hand in my life. About six years later He gave me a closer look.

I was thirty-seven years old when He planted this next seed. My wife and I were at Group Health Hospital in Bellevue, Washington. We both had a job to do. My job was to help Pam remember to breathe, and to time her contractions. Pam's job was to give birth to our first (and only) child. Pam didn't seem to be enjoying her job; I was ecstatic about mine.

I'll never forget how natural it all seemed to be—no, how "intended" it all seemed to be. A new life was coming into the world. The breathing, the contractions, even the pain, all seemed to be part of some grand design. I marveled at this miracle unfolding before me. Then the nurse called for the doctor to hurry. We rushed into the delivery room, barely in time. Moments later the doctor gently placed this new life, my daughter, in the cradle of my arms. Six pounds twelve ounces, nineteen inches long, she was for me in that moment the entire universe. Gazing on her angelic face I experienced a love so intense that I could not imagine ever knowing a greater love. I remember at the time thinking I would gladly give my life for hers. Now, more than thirty years later, I would still give my life for hers; yet I have since experienced a far greater love.

I look back now and can recognize many times when God planted seeds of faith in my life. But that emerging faith didn't begin to take clear form until I was approaching my mid-forties.

One of my co-workers walked into the office one day and announced that the county prosecutor was filing a lawsuit against her husband. Her husband had signed a petition requesting a referendum on a growth management plan that the county council was considering for adoption. The county took the position that the proposed plan was in compliance with a state statute and that a county referendum was not applicable. The county prosecutor called each person who had signed the petition and threatened to sue them personally if they didn't withdraw their names. My co-worker was frightened. I was outraged. So I embraced the cause and immersed myself in politics.

It was not just this threatened trampling of the right to referendum guaranteed in our state's constitution that bothered me. Over the past 20 years I had watched a number of disturbing changes take place in our society. People had begun suing each other over anything and everything. If someone spilled hot coffee in their lap they sued the café that sold it to them. If they fell down the stairs they sued the contractor that constructed the building. Everything was somebody else's fault. Moreover, crime rates, divorce rates and illegitimate birth rates had all increased over 1000% since I had graduated from high school. Government couldn't seem to pass laws fast enough, and yet people clamored for more laws. We couldn't seem to surrender our liberty fast enough. Yet all these additional laws appeared to do nothing to curb the escalating chaos and suffering in our society.

This particular referendum dispute raised a number of constitutional issues. So I re-read the Constitution of the United States, and then began reading other writings by our founding fathers. Two things struck me. First, these men were indisputably bright, learned, with wisdom and foresight far beyond the ordinary. Secondly, these men were indisputably Christians—devout, committed Christians. Something

5

was wrong with this picture; I had assumed Christians were naïve and unworldly. A faint, nagging suspicion began to emerge. If brilliant visionaries like our founding fathers could believe in a Christian God, maybe there existed some logic that had escaped me. That vague suspicion began to float around the edge of my consciousness. But another idea emerged that was even stronger. It was becoming more and more evident to me that it wasn't simply a political crisis this nation was facing. *It was some kind of spiritual crisis.* Neither Republicans nor Democrats were going to solve our problems. These issues ran to the very core of who we are as human beings.

I didn't know it yet, but this glimpse into the mystery of our increasingly chaotic world was the beginning of a spiritual awakening in my life. It was also God's way of preparing me to meet the Blackmores.

᠕

"For our struggle is not against flesh and blood, but against the rulers, against the authorities, against the powers of this dark world and against the spiritual forces of evil in the heavenly realms."

EPHESIANS 6:12

Chapter Two

The Decision

I was now forty-five years old. Pam and I were sitting in the living room of some new acquaintances, a retired couple that lived just a couple of blocks down the street. We were discussing real estate. This couple, Ralph and Gloria Blackmore, were thinking about selling one of the many rental properties they had bought and managed over the years. Pam and I were interested. The property's financial records were spread out on the coffee table in front of us.

In the middle of this business discussion, Gloria, out of the blue, leaned forward and asked me a question absurdly unrelated to the topic at hand. "Do you know Jesus Christ as your personal Lord and Savior?" she asked. I panicked. "Oh no," I thought, "a Holy Roller" (at that time my disparaging label for all fervent, vocal Christians). While I firmly supported people's right to believe anything they wanted, I also felt strongly that they should keep their religious beliefs to themselves. I had zero patience for evangelists.

Normally I would have responded with something like, "Look, I'm not a Christian and I'm not really interested, so let's not even go there." But seeds of faith had previously been sown, and a curious call skirted the edge of my consciousness. Besides, these were obviously intelligent, successful, astute business people. They ran their business to turn a profit. My distorted image of a Christian was someone who was poor and wanted those who made money to give it to those who didn't. Somehow Ralph and Gloria didn't fit that distorted personal bias. Yet I was still surprised to hear myself answer, "No, I don't know Jesus. What about him?"

So Ralph and Gloria began to tell me about Jesus. Not about Christianity, mind you. Not about a church. Not about theology or some dogma. They talked about a person—a person they seemed to know personally, and loved with childlike transparency. I found myself curiously attracted to their story. And since they started this conversation, I also felt justified in asking some tough questions. How could a "God" who supposedly created and loves mankind allow such pain and suffering? How could a God who is at the same time all-knowing and all-powerful allow some innocent single working mother to walk in the path of a drunk driver? How could Jesus' death on the cross redeem mankind? How could Jesus and His Father be one in the same person? How could God send people to hell just because Christianity didn't make sense to them? Nothing about Christianity made sense to me. There had to be hundreds of millions of people with the same doubts. Apparently hell was going to be a very busy place. My questions ran on and on.

Ralph and Gloria seemed to know a lot about God, and the Bible. They joyfully and enthusiastically responded to each question. But quite frankly, their answers were not convincing. Still...I did have to grudgingly admit that their answers were at least somewhat plausible. In fact, I began to realize, they were too plausible to ignore. Later that night at home, as Pam slept beside me, I found myself unable to sleep, replaying the evening's conversation over and over in my head.

I couldn't let it go. Oddly, I felt like I was being *called* to make a decision. To my great consternation, I even felt drawn to decide for Christ. But that was a decision that intellectually I could not make. How could one actually *know* that God really existed? How could one actually *know* that Jesus is the Christ, the Savior of mankind? No one had seen Him in 2000 years (or so I assumed). No one had even heard from Him in 2000 years (or again, so I assumed). So how could anyone honestly profess "I believe" when there could be no way to truly know? For me to acknowledge Jesus as Lord would be intellectually dishonest. Yet according to Ralph and Gloria it was absolutely necessary to believe in Jesus, to accept Him as Lord and Savior, in order to attain salvation. They said if I professed with my mouth "Jesus is Lord," and believed in my heart that God raised Him from the dead, I would be saved. But how could one *believe* that which one had no way of *knowing*?

I saw no way through this dilemma. But still I couldn't let it go. For two thousand years, apparently highly intelligent people had found a way to believe in Him. What was the answer?

During this tortured contemplation, a comment that Gloria had made earlier kept coming to mind. At one point that evening Gloria had stated, quite matter-of-factly, "God always answers prayer." For some reason that simple statement of faith kept inserting itself into my thoughts. Over and over, "God *always* answers prayer." Finally it dawned on me. Maybe that was the key. If God's desire was for me to be saved, as the Blackmores had stated; if my salvation was predicated on belief and acceptance of Jesus Christ as my Lord and Savior; if God did always answer prayer; then perhaps therein lay the answer. Faith had to somehow be God's job, not mine. If I did acknowledge Christ as my Savior, and then asked God for the faith to believe it, He would have to provide the faith—right? That is, if He actually existed, if He

9

actually desired my salvation, and if He actually answered prayer. A lot of "ifs", but what did I have to lose? So I made a decision. I would surrender my life to Christ, fully and sincerely. Then, if a year later, I had no more certainty of God's existence than I had at that moment, no personal experience of Christ in my life, I could look back on it as an interesting experiment. It would cost me nothing. But conversely, if the Blackmores were right, doing nothing could cost me all eternity.

So I prayed as simply and as honestly as I could, "Jesus, I don't know you. But I will simply accept that you are who people say you are. I accept that you are the Son of God, one in being with God; that you died on the cross for my sins; that you arose from the dead, and that through faith in you I too will be raised to eternal life. Jesus, I can't even imagine how many times I've offended you. I am truly sorry. But I ask you now to come into my heart and be the Lord of my life. Everything I am, and everything I could ever hope to be, I surrender to you."

Then for the first time in my life I asked God for a favor. "Father in heaven, my prayer is this, give me faith. Make me believe that which I've just professed. I can't see any way to be sure you even exist unless you do something. In Jesus' Name. Amen."

The struggle was over. I drifted off to sleep.

◡◠

"For it is by grace you have been saved, through faith—and this not from yourselves, it is the gift of God—not by works, so that no one can boast."

EPHESIANS 2:8

10

Chapter Three
_____

God Always Answers Prayer

The First Miracle

Waking up the next morning I felt nothing different or unusual, except perhaps a moment of panic as I recalled the decision made the night before; "Bill, have you lost your mind?", I wondered. "What were you thinking last night?" But acknowledging that I *had* made that decision, I reasoned I had better learn more about this person Jesus, and about Christianity. On the bookshelf I found a Bible that someone had given me a year or two earlier (my childhood Bible had long since disappeared). Since it was Christ I had professed the night before, it seemed like a good idea to start with the New Testament. The New Testament was, according to the Blackmores, a record of the new Covenant that God had established through Jesus. During breakfast I opened to Matthew 1:1, the first verse of the New Testament, and began to read.

While *I* didn't feel different, it became immediately evident to me that *the Bible* had somehow changed. In the past the Bible had struck me as both irrelevant and illogical. It had always read like ancient mythology, mixed with a spattering of equally ancient history—just unsophisticated and pre-scientific minds trying to explain the struggles in their world. I had never found the stories believable or the message supportable. And the whole concept of sin and redemption seemed absurd. Yet this morning that previous perception changed. Somehow the Bible came alive. It began to make sense—transformed from the disconnected musings of ancient men to a contemporary, relevant, magnetic…what? The Blackmores had referred to the Bible as the *Word of God*. That was it. Reading the Bible this particular morning was not like reading a book. It was more like standing in God's presence while he patiently explained the order of the universe. Remarkably, His explanations were beginning to strike a chord. I wanted to hear more. I didn't want to put it down. But regrettably, I had to get to work.

Carefully marking my place with a bookmark, I reflected on this surprising transformation. In the past I had found the Bible agonizingly illogical, clearly irrelevant, and painfully boring to read. Now it was actually making sense, and I couldn't turn the pages fast enough. How could this be? How could my perception of this book change so radically, so instantly? I could think of one possibility. A few hours earlier I had made a decision to acknowledge Jesus Christ as my Lord and Savior. I had submitted my life to Him and had asked God to reveal Himself to me. Could that be it? Was this a supernatural experience—a revelation and experience of God?

I took the Bible to work with me and spent the lunch hour reading it. I opened it again as soon as I returned home from work. It drew me into its message with inexplicable attraction, with irresistible power. This book was not just about events thousands of years ago. It was about what was happening in our world even at that moment. It was about the daily events of my generation, the struggles, the pain, the victories and the joy. It was about me, my family, my community, my nation, my world, and my time in history. Simultaneously, it was about all people and all time. It was about war and peace, good and evil, love and hate. It was about a spiritual battle that had been raging from time immemorial. It clarified the struggles and brought rationality to a seemingly irrational world. It provided truth. How I knew it was true I could not say. But I *knew*. This was *the* Truth.

That evening we met again with Ralph and Gloria. I announced that I had surrendered my life to Christ the night before. They were elated at the news. Then I asked a favor. Ralph had mentioned that he was leading a weekly evening Bible study. I asked him if I could attend. His answer was an emphatic "yes!" I could hardly wait. All week long I looked forward to that Bible study like a twelve year old looks forward to Christmas morning. And I immersed myself in the Bible during every spare moment.

The Second Miracle

Previous to this new awakening in my life I had always found outspoken Christians irritating. Folks who found "miracles" in every unusual event annoyed me. Christians who publicly, enthusiastically proclaimed praise for God annoyed me even more. Uninvited evangelizing was in my view an unacceptable invasion of my privacy, often evoking from me a curt reply. I'm embarrassed to admit that I had often referred to fervent, vocal Christians as "Bible Thumpers" or "Holy Rollers." At the time I considered these labels to be disparaging. That was my sole intention for using them.

I don't know what I expected to find at Ralph's Bible study, but I wasn't prepared for the scene that unfolded before me. Ralph and Gloria lived in a multi-million-dollar home overlooking the bay. Yet the street address they gave me for the study was someone's double wide modular home in a retirement park. Remember my previously admitted bias about Christians and money? All the fervent Christians I happened to know personally were of extremely modest income. What would I find on the other side of this door?

Entering the home, my worst fears were confirmed. I was confronted with about a dozen men and women of various ages who were, I immediately realized, the Holy Rollers of all Holy Rollers!

"Praise the Lord," someone exclaimed, "He's here!" Ralph and Gloria had obviously made known my profession of Christ. They crowded around me. They invited me in and hugged me. They congratulated me. They praised the Lord—repeatedly. Then they began sharing all the other "miracles" they had personally experienced that week. These folks scared the life out of me! Mercifully, Ralph called the Bible study to order. But then, to my horror, he began by praying—*actually talking to God out loud right in front of everyone.* Were we all going to have to do that? I was mortified.

My inclination was to bolt. I didn't think I could endure a night surrounded by all these fanatics. But then inexplicably, as the evening proceeded, an amazing calm began to settle over me. I began to experience a growing affection for these people, an unexplainable attraction. I began to feel as if I were with close family members. The truth is, I was. By God's grace I was tangibly experiencing the intimate relationship that exists within the family of believers, the family that the Bible calls the Body of Christ (Romans 12:4-5).

As I drove home that night I marveled at the second unmistakable transformation of the week. If I had blundered into that group two weeks earlier I would have excused myself and escaped as quickly as possible. But not only did I not flee, in minutes I felt completely calm, completely at peace, completely...what? At home. I felt like I had come home; that I was exactly where I was always intended to be. What could have caused that dramatic transformation and that inexplicable sense of well-being? What had changed? The inescapable conclusion was that five days earlier I had invited Jesus Christ to be Lord of my life. Something supernatural was happening in my life. It had to be related to that decision and to my prayer, "Father, give me faith. Make me believe that which I've just professed." God was answering prayer.

∽

"I tell you the truth, my Father will give you whatever you ask in my name. Until now you have not asked for anything in my name. Ask and you will receive, and your joy will be complete."

JOHN 16:24

The Third Miracle

I relate this third miracle reluctantly, as it involves a very personal medical condition. But because this miracle was also integral to God's revelation of Himself to me in those first weeks, I feel compelled to share it.

The early 80's were tough years in our household. Pam and I were newly married. I made my living as a carpenter/carpenter foreman, but work opportunities were becoming scarce. Inflation had begun to soar and the national economy was gripped in a recession. Interest rates had climbed into double digits, crippling the construction industry. With interest rates so inflated, few could afford to buy houses or finance new commercial projects. I spent months and months searching for permanent employment, with no success. The few projects that were being built were not hiring, sometimes even displaying crude signs spray-painted on sheets of plywood announcing "not hiring, don't ask." In those pre-computer days, "door to door" visits of construction

15

sites and contractors' offices were the common ways of finding positions in the construction industry. Yet in that protracted and devastating recession it wasn't uncommon to be greeted with grim laughter when inquiring about open positions. The continual rejection during my futile job search, and the building financial pressures in our household, became crushing burdens that devastated my self-esteem.

One evening after a particularly difficult and frustratingly non-productive day of job searching, I felt as if something inside snapped. The next morning, a trip to the bathroom turned the toilet bowl bright red with blood. Later that day I experienced another bloody bowel movement. I called our family doctor. His immediate concern, as was mine, was colon cancer. We scheduled an examination for his earliest opening.

Following a series of examinations by my family doctor and some specialists, the doctors diagnosed the problem as ulcerative colitis, a disease of the colon that allows blood to enter the colon through ulcers in the wall of the colon. The causes of this condition are not definitively known, but stress often seems to be a contributing factor. While not a life-threatening condition in itself, UC does make one more prone to colon cancer.

Relieved that I didn't have cancer, I was none the less disturbed by the fact that I was now bleeding recurrently, experiencing two or three bloody bowel movements per day. The doctors prescribed some medicines intended to alleviate the symptoms, but with no apparent effect. I tolerated the bleeding a few more months, and then made another appointment. My doctor then prescribed some different medicines, which again gave no relief from the symptoms. Thus began a cycle that continued for several years. I would put up with the condition for months, grow disgusted, then in desperation try another visit to the doctor and another round of various medicines, always without success. Even after the economy recovered and the stress lifted, the bleeding persisted.

In the twelfth year of this annual cycle, I once again reached a point where I felt I just had to find some medical relief for this ongoing condition. I again made an appointment with my family doctor, who happened to be booked several weeks out. It was a week before that scheduled appointment that I sat down with Ralph and Gloria Blackmore to negotiate a real estate purchase, and instead accepted Jesus Christ as my Lord and Savior.

At my doctor's appointment the week following my decision to accept Christ, the physician prescribed yet another medication. This medicine came in suppository form, which I found particularly repulsive. Later at home, looking at those menacing capsules, I made a decision. Throwing the pills into the trash bin, I sat down and did something I would never have thought to do a couple of weeks earlier: I prayed. "Lord, I will no longer put my trust in man to heal me of this illness. I surrender this condition to You. I ask for You to heal me. I believe You can do it. But if it is not Your will, then I willingly accept living with this condition the rest of my life. I pray this in Jesus' name, amen."

The bleeding stopped immediately! It has now been over twenty-five years since I prayed that prayer, and the condition has never returned.

I was thrilled that Jesus had answered my prayer. But the full implication of this miracle didn't strike home until a few days later when I came across an account in the Bible of Jesus healing a woman, who like me, had suffered bleeding for twelve continuous years, with no relief from the medical profession of her day. This same Jesus, who intervened in her life 2000 years ago, had just intervened in mine in an identical fashion! The Truth was inescapable. Not only does Jesus really exist, but He continues to interact personally and powerfully with us, even today!

"A large crowd followed and pressed around him. And a woman was there who had been subject to bleeding for twelve years. She had suffered a great deal under the care of many doctors and had spent all she had, yet instead of getting better she grew worse. When she heard about Jesus, she came up behind him in the crowd and touched his cloak, because she thought, 'If I just touch his clothes, I will be healed.' Immediately her bleeding stopped and she felt in her body that she was freed from her suffering.

At once Jesus realized that power had gone out from him. He turned around and asked, 'Who touched my clothes?'

'You see the people crowded against you,' his disciples answered, 'and yet you can ask, "Who touched me?"'

But Jesus kept looking around to see who had done it. Then the woman, knowing what had happened to her, came and fell at his feet and, trembling with fear, told him the whole truth. He said to her, 'Daughter, your faith has healed you. Go in peace and be freed from your suffering.'"

MARK 5:24-34

Chapter Four

The Journey

In the weeks (and years) that followed, I read the Bible every spare moment. I had a hunger for the Word of God that was simply insatiable. I devoured Matthew, the first book of the New Testament, and then quickly moved on to the other Gospels. Since Ralph's class was a detailed study of the Book of Revelation, I also skipped ahead and began concurrently reading Revelation, the last book of the New Testament. I actually began reading it in three places. I began at the beginning of Revelation in an effort to catch up with the class, and at the place they were studying when I joined the group. I also read ahead to try to prepare for each week's class. My Bible had bookmarks protruding everywhere.

The people in the study group couldn't have been nicer or more supportive. They were clearly excited that I, a 45-year old man, had just surrendered my life to Christ and had been *saved*, to use their terminology. Their concern for the souls of others amazed me. They loved strangers with a love that was inexplicable. How could anyone love total strangers or care so deeply for their souls? Not realizing it yet, I was witnessing the love and presence of Christ Himself, expressed through

His Body, the Church. God was beginning to show me His face. He was becoming more and more real in my consciousness and in my life.

While my new friends were clearly excited about my conversion, they became perhaps equally excited when they found out my wife was Catholic. They were going to *save* her also, although they didn't reveal that to me immediately. (I was not yet aware of the theological differences between Catholics and Protestants.) They urged me to invite Pam to the study. So I did. Pam was a little suspicious of this group of Christians. She was a cradle Catholic and had very little experience with Christians from other denominations. But she was witnessing a dramatic and welcomed transformation in me. So after a few weeks she decided to try the class as well.

My new friends were as kind and generous to Pam as they were to me. But it became obvious they were concerned about her eternal salvation. Had she accepted Christ as her personal Lord and Savior? Did she have a saving relationship with Jesus or was she, in their view, erringly trying to gain heaven through good works or through the rituals of the Catholic Church? She was becoming increasingly uncomfortable with the implications of their attention.

By this time I had read through the New Testament at least once and had begun each week attending Mass at my wife's Catholic church, in addition to a weekly service with friends at an Evangelical Protestant church. I was truly a novice Christian with much to learn. But I had one experience that the more mature members of the Bible study did not have. I actually attended Catholic Mass and heard first-hand the teachings of the Catholic Church expressed from the pulpit. From my perspective, there was essentially no *practical* difference between what Protestants and Catholics were teaching regarding our salvation (more on that later). It seemed to me that my Bible study friends held some misconceptions about what Catholics believed.

Opportunely (or providentially), the priest at Pam's church felt moved to insert copies of his sermons in the weekly bulletin (I found out later that this was the only time in his life that he had ever published a sermon). I brought copies of each of the two consecutive sermons he had published to the Bible study. I showed them to Ralph after the study was over and asked what he thought of the teaching. He read both sermons carefully, then marveled at what a gifted and accurate teaching each sermon represented. He had only one criticism. As Ralph put it, the pastor laid out a great table, but at the end of the sermons he should have invited the congregation to partake—he should have ended his sermons with an "altar call," an invitation to make a conscious decision to surrender their lives to Christ. Had I understood the Mass better at that time, I could have explained that the Celebration of the Eucharist for Catholics—the receiving of Communion, is in at least one sense an altar call. Our attitude, as we approach the altar to receive the Eucharist, is supposed to be one of surrender to Him whom we are about to receive under the appearance of bread and wine. My own understanding would come later. But as it was, I noticed the tone of the group began to change. They began talking less about saving Catholics and more about the "revival" that appeared to be taking place in the Catholic Church.

Even at this very early period of our relationship I was experiencing God in a very real sense. His Word, the Bible, had come alive for me. Jesus, His Son, was a person I was aware of in prayer, in the Bible, and in worship. He was tangible. When I sat quietly praying to Jesus, I felt His presence fill the room. I was not alone. When I prayed to God the Father, His presence filled not only the room, but the universe and beyond, enveloping me and drawing me into His infinite nature. I had yet to tangibly experience the Holy Spirit, but that was about to change in a remarkable way.

"No one comes to the Father except through me. If you really knew me, you would know my Father as well. From now on, you do know him and have seen him."

JOHN 14: 6-7.

"All of this I have spoken while still with you. But the Counselor, the Holy Spirit, whom the Father will send in my name, will teach you all things and will remind you of everything I have said to you."

JOHN 14:25-26

The Holy Spirit

Vern Clark took pity on me. Vern was also a student in Ralph's Bible study, although by no means a rookie. Vern had been studying the Bible for forty years. Like Ralph and Gloria, he was an Evangelical Pentecostal Christian (although at that time I didn't know a Pentecostal from a Jehovah's Witness). Ralph's Bible study looked at each verse of the Book of Revelation and then related it back to prophecy in the Old Testament. I hadn't even begun reading the Old Testament yet—I didn't know Abraham from Zechariah. This study was proving to be quite a challenge.

Vern approached me after Bible study one evening and asked if I would like to study the Old Testament with him. He offered to tutor me in his home one night a week. I was elated.

So one night the following week I sat down on a couch in Vern's living room. Vern prayed that God would open our hearts and minds to His Word, and then began reading at Genesis 1:1, the opening verse of the Old Testament. He would read out loud, stopping occasionally to highlight some pertinent point or to answer one of my frequent questions. Each week we followed the same process. When his voice grew tired, I would read aloud. Vern knew a great deal about the theological positions of many of the various Christian denominations and he shared openly with me. My awareness of God and my understanding of Christian thought continued to grow. God's heart was becoming ever clearer to me.

I look back at that time and marvel at God's hand in my life. A few weeks before I couldn't tolerate fervent Christians, found reading the Bible insufferable, and dreaded going to church. Now I was going to two churches each Sunday, attending two Bible studies each week, reading the Bible every spare moment, praying constantly, and my new best friends were Holy Rollers! My wife couldn't believe the change, but she loved it! What was happening to me? What could have brought about such radical change? Surely, it had to be Jesus. I had committed my life to Him as He calls us to do. He in turn began to fulfill His promises. He was about to fulfill His promise to send the Holy Spirit.

I don't recall how long I had been studying with Vern—I don't think more than a few weeks. Then one evening as I sat down on his couch to begin Bible study, he casually dropped this bomb: "God told me to pray for you for the baptism of the Holy Spirit," Vern stated in a matter-of-fact tone. "Do you know what the baptism of the Holy Spirit is?" he continued. I thought I could remember reading something about the baptism of the Holy Spirit in the New Testament. But what astounded me was his statement "God told me..." It had never occurred to me that God still spoke to people on earth. I didn't know what to say, other than if he thought that was what God wanted, it was okay with me.

He didn't pray immediately, but instead began the Bible study. So I assumed he had meant he would pray for me privately during his daily prayer time. But at the end of the study when I stood to leave he asked if he could pray for me before I left. I said okay. He then surprised me by placing both his hands firmly on the top of my head, something I had never seen or experienced before. Praying out loud, he said, "In the name of Jesus, receive the baptism of the Holy Spirit." He then commanded me to receive the gifts of the Spirit, and named several gifts specifically, including wisdom, knowledge, healing, tongues, and other gifts. The prayer lasted less than a minute, concluding with his "Amen." I echoed "Amen," and it was done.

I felt really awkward. I thanked Vern for his prayer but asked him not to be too disappointed if nothing happened. I told him I really had never thought about the gifts of the Spirit before; I was still just trying to get to know Jesus. And in fact, I told him, I didn't really feel anything as he prayed. Vern responded that I needn't worry about it; that it's all up to God. But he also informed me that God gives us gifts to use. If we won't use them, then we lose them. So Vern recommended that if I did feel "called" to use one of the gifts, such as a sense to pray for someone who was ill, to be obedient in faith and do it. Then simply trust the outcome to God.

I remember thinking to myself as I walked out to the car, "Man; that was weird!" I climbed into the car, turned the key, and started to pull away from the curb. As I did I began feeling a pressure building in the back of my throat, almost as if the back of my tongue was swelling up. I swallowed a couple of times, but the pressure increased. It felt like something was trying to get out. I opened my mouth and spoke. To my utter amazement, these strange foreign words came out. Not only were they from a foreign language, they were in a completely foreign intonation—something like an Asian dialect, but different. Kind of like a chant, but different. I was stunned. But more stunning than that unknown language was the emotion I experienced as those words were spoken. I felt an overwhelming sense of joy erupting from somewhere deep inside, like a bubble rising from the depths of the ocean, a place so deep within me that I had not even been aware that place existed. I paused for a moment in amazement, and then I spoke again. With the second yielding to this inexplicable impulse, the floodgates opened. Suddenly I found myself driving down the street, overwhelmed with this limitless outpouring of joy, praising God in a language I'm sure I'd never heard before. I don't know what the words meant literally. But I did know they were an expression of an otherwise inexpressible joy and love for God; an outpouring of praise greater than any I could articulate in my native language. It was the Holy Spirit speaking through me. It was what the Bible calls the gift of tongues.

With one hand on the steering wheel and one hand raised in worship to God, I praised Him in this newfound prayer language all the way home. I must have looked crazy to other motorists. When I pulled up in front of my house I couldn't will myself to stop. So I continued down to a nearby park and sat in the car for another hour, praising God in that mysterious language, overwhelmed with joy in the Lord.

It was now so late when I returned home that I didn't have time to open the Bible to read about what had just happened to me. It wasn't until after work the next day that I found time alone to read. I opened the Bible to 1 Corinthians, Chapter 12, where Vern had told me God spoke about these particular gifts......

Allow me to pause here to emphasize how intimately God knows each of us. Knowing myself (and God knows me much better) I expect that if I had received this gift of tongues at some emotion-charged charismatic conference, or during a moving Pentecostal prayer meeting, surrounded by other people praying in tongues, I would have later wondered if this was truly a work of God. Being the pragmatist that I am, I would have eventually questioned whether this experience was authentic, or just an emotional reaction to environmental influences. But the undeniable reality was that I had experienced no such environmental influences. Not only had I never experienced any prompting or desire to speak in tongues, I didn't even know what "tongues" were. Rather, a fellow Christian acted in faithful obedience to God and simply prayed for me. Surely this had to be from God.

But God wanted to make sure I never doubted that this was a gift from Him. That next evening, when I opened the Bible and began to read the passage about the gifts of the Spirit, *God magnified those words in my sight*. Literally lifted and hovering above the page, the words became magnified five times the size of the surrounding text. As the miracle of those magnified words burned into my vision, the miracle of God's astounding love and His intimate interest in each of us individually, burned into my heart. This God, who created countless billions of stars and held them in place by the Word of His mouth, took His time to demonstrate His personal interest in *me*. How could that be? Who was I to the Creator of the universe? Yet God cared about me—*personally*. What intimate, amazing grace!

＊

"When they arrived, they prayed for them that
they might receive the Holy Spirit, because the
Holy Spirit had not yet come upon any of them;
they had simply been baptized into the name of
the Lord Jesus. Then Peter and John placed their
hands on them, and they received the Holy Spirit."

ACTS 8:15-17

The Love of God

I had been a Christian for only a few months when a relatively new evangelical organization called *Promise Keepers* held a conference at the Kingdome in Seattle, WA (the former stadium of the Seattle Seahawks). I talked to some guys I knew at the Catholic Church I attended with Pam. Five of us decided to ride down together. I also invited a friend from the Protestant church I attended. We had a full car.

About 60,000 men packed the stadium that weekend. For a day and a half several ministers from around the country led us in worship and in commitment to our responsibilities as Christian men. Most memorable to me that weekend was God's overwhelmingly tangible presence. You could literally touch that Presence filling the stadium. At any moment one could look around the stadium and see men weeping with joy and conviction, being transformed before one's eyes. It was a life changing experience.

Driving home from the conference, we all discussed which message most touched our hearts. For each of us it was something different. For me it was the call to reconciliation in the church — reconciliation between denominations and between races. To this day that has remained for me an essential understanding of God's desire for his Church.

However, I discovered from this event, and from other conferences that I've attended, that God often later reveals important principles that go beyond first impressions. Such was the case after this first conference. I was sure God's central message to me was His desire for reconciliation in the Church. However, when I began prayer the next morning, God overpowered me with an even greater revelation. Sitting in my living room in the quiet of the early morning, I became increasingly aware of God's great love for each of us. Growing in intensity, I began to experience God's love for me *personally*, pouring over me in waves, literally like ocean waves washing up onto a beach. I slid off the couch onto my knees. Wave after wave of love washed over me, physically rocking me back on my heels. Then, like waves running back to the ocean after reaching the uppermost limits of the beach, I began to experience waves of love coming from my heart, rushing back to God. His love would wash over me, and my love would run back to him; it was a love unimaginably intense. Then I thought back to the day my daughter was born and the love I experienced for her. I recalled that as I had held her in my arms for the first time, I had thought I would never experience a greater love. I had been wrong. On this morning, my experience of God's love surpassed anything I could have ever imagined, even my profound love for my daughter.

The intensity of God's love continued to swell, wave after wave growing in size and power, until finally I could withstand no more. Falling over on my side I cried out "Please, God! Relent! I can't endure the fullness of your love!" God's love for each of us is infinitely beyond what any human mind could imagine or comprehend.

As He had done so many times already, God was again revealing His existence, His presence, and His nature. He was continuing to answer that first prayer for faith.

مر

"God is love."

1 JOHN 4:16

I am who I AM

One afternoon in late July or early August of 1996, I received a call from my father. Dad said he'd been to the doctor that day. The doctor had received the results of some tests taken earlier. Dad had lung cancer; an aggressive type. The doctor predicted Dad would live only six more months. Dad was just 67 years old.

Dad's health had been poor for years. He was a life-long smoker, already suffering severely from emphysema. I had been expecting for some time that this day would come. Still, my heart was broken because I knew that Dad had no relationship with Jesus Christ. Although his mother was a devout Catholic, for some reason as a young teenager Dad had rejected the Church and Christ. All my life he refused to even listen to anyone talk about Christianity. Now he was dying. The truth I saw as Dad discussed his impending death was my father approaching an eternal separation from God through his rejection of Christ—an eternity in hell. I was desperate to rescue him. I had to tell him about Jesus.

So I asked him if I could come over to see him that evening. He said "sure."

Throughout the 3-hour drive to my parents' home in Port Angeles, WA, I struggled with what I might say; with how I might broach the subject. I was terrified that I would blow it and that Dad would not respond, or that he would not even let me talk to him about Jesus at all. Never had I felt such a burden; that so much was at stake. It was not just a life at stake. It was an eternal life, and even more, the eternal life of someone I loved dearly. I prayed fervently that God would prepare Dad's heart and guide my words.

It was dark by the time I arrived at my parents' house. In spite of my prayer and my rehearsal during the three hour trip, I felt woefully inadequate. I picked up my cell phone and called Dave Alcorta, a friend and brother in my *Promise Keepers* men's group, and now a Deacon in the Catholic Church. I briefly explained the situation to him and then we prayed together. Finally, I walked up the front stairs and rang the doorbell.

After greeting and visiting briefly with Mom and Dad, Mom went to the kitchen to leave Dad and me alone together to talk. Dad explained in greater detail the test results and prognosis. The doctor said that he could undergo radiation treatments if he chose, but that they could prolong his life for only a short period of time, if at all. Dad had already decided to forgo treatment and live his last months in as much physical comfort as possible. I concurred. We talked a while longer. Finally I knew I couldn't delay any longer. I had to talk to him about Jesus.

When I recall how I broached the subject it sounds even sillier to me today than it did then in my desperation. I just didn't know how to start, so this is what I said: "Dad, they say you won't find any atheists in foxholes. You must realize you're in a foxhole. I want to talk to you about God's plan of salvation. I want to talk to you about Jesus." To my surprise and to my eternal gratitude to God, Dad said, "OK."

So to the best of my ability I shared the gospel with Dad, of salvation through faith in our Lord Jesus Christ. Then Dad began to ask questions, many of the same questions I had asked only a couple of years earlier. For an hour or more I answered his questions as well as I could. Finally, when he seemed to run out of things to ask, he said, "Bill, I don't know, but I will think about it." My response was quite calm, far calmer than I was feeling inside. I said "Ok, Dad," and left it at that. But inside I was singing for joy, praising God and thanking him for the work he was doing in Dad, because I remembered the promise that God had given us through the Prophet Isaiah. God had said "my word will not return to me empty, but will accomplish what I desire and achieve the purpose for which I sent it" (Isaiah 55:11). Dad had received God's Word, had searched God's Word, and had promised to reflect on God's Word. I was absolutely certain that with six months still to live, between Jesus and me, we were going to get my Dad saved.

But as it turned out Dad didn't have 6 months.

Dad appeared no sicker during a following visit a couple of weeks later. Then after only two more weeks had passed, I received a call from Mom. She sounded frightened. Dad was not doing well. He was having trouble speaking, slurring his words. He was losing his balance, stumbling frequently. I said I'd drive over that day.

Mom had not exaggerated. When I arrived, it became immediately obvious to me that Dad was failing rapidly. That afternoon Mom went out in the back yard to do something, leaving Dad and me sitting alone at the kitchen table. I knew time was very short.

I asked Dad if he wanted me to call a priest. He shook his head "no." Dad had been away from the Church so long that the priesthood held no meaning for him. So I asked him if I could pray with him. Dad shook his head "yes." So while Dad sat with eyes closed, leaning forward with his elbows on the table and his head resting in his hands, I prayed out loud what Evangelicals call the "sinner's prayer." I told Jesus that we accepted that he was the Lord, the Son of God, Savior and King. I told Jesus that we acknowledged his lordship and authority in our own lives, that we surrendered ourselves completely to Him. I asked Him to come into our hearts and be our Lord and Savior. I asked His forgiveness for the times we offended Him. I asked for His mercy and salvation.

Mom came back in just as I finished this short prayer. During the prayer, Dad had shown no outward sign of response. I wanted to pray with him again and to ask if he accepted that prayer as his own. I wanted to be sure, but we were out of time.

Relatives began arriving that evening. The next morning a woman from hospice visited and explained the situation. Dad was dying and his organs were shutting down one at a time, reserving energy for the most essential organs until the end. She said he'd drift into a coma within a day or so and die within a week. Dad mumbled that he wanted to die at home, not in a nursing facility. So hospice agreed to have a hospital bed dropped off at my parents' house and to show me how to care for Dad. I agreed to stay and do so.

The next day hospice set up the hospital bed in the living room (neither of the two bedrooms in the small house were large enough to hold an extra bed). By then Dad could barely speak or walk. We helped him into bed, where over the next couple of days he slipped into a deep coma. His body became as lifeless and leaden as a fallen log. The only sign of life was his wheezy, laborious breathing.

I spent much of the next two or three days praying, reading the Bible, visiting with Mom, and attending to Dad. One afternoon I was sitting on the couch in the living room. Dad lay comatose on the hospital bed before me, his head to the left, feet to the right. The September sun was casting a soft glow in the room. I sat on the couch praying, not about anything in particular. I was just spending time with my earthly father and with my heavenly Father.

As I prayed, my eyes rested idly on Dad lying before me. Suddenly, to my shock and amazement, Dad sat up. Not his body, but his spirit. Then, taking hold of the handrails on either side of the bed, Dad's spirit slid off the foot of the bed and stood up. My first thought was that I must have fallen asleep and was dreaming. I even pinched myself. But I was clearly wide-awake. My second thought was that perhaps Dad was dying and I was witnessing his spirit leave his body. But why and how could I see his spirit? Was God somehow stirring in me some dormant ability to see spirits? For what purpose? My thoughts began to blur in confusion and shock.

Then an even more shocking event occurred. Suddenly, without warning, my own spirit leaned forward out of my body, stood up, and walked over to my father. I watched in paralyzing astonishment as our two spirits begin speaking to one another, although I was deaf to the sound of our voices. My brain felt numb and frozen at the sight of my spirit leaving my body. It seemed nothing could be more amazing.

I then caught movement to my right. Shifting my gaze in that direction, I watched Jesus walk through the door into the living room—not His body, but His Spirit. I recognized Him instantly.

Jesus walked directly to my father and me and I could see Him begin speaking, although I could not hear His voice either. I watched our spirits respond. The three of us stood in conversation, our expressions intent, but not unsettled. My own thoughts came with difficulty, chaotically. Through the confusion the thought "communion" kept coming to mind. Not knowing what we were discussing, I still sensed somehow that the three of us were in communion.

Then one overwhelmingly powerful thought exploded in my mind, cutting through the chaos with stunning clarity. The thought was this: *"My Word will not return to me empty."* The words resounded in my mind like a cymbal. It was the Word that God had spoken through the prophet Isaiah. I realized God had also just spoken this Word to me. I began to wonder; was God allowing me to witness the completion of the conversion of my father?

The three of us talked a short while longer and then each spirit returned from whence it came. I sat afterward in stunned silence, trying to make sense of the incredible event I had just witnessed.

Was it really God's purpose through this revelation to allow me to witness the fulfillment of my father's conversion? It seemed to be so, yet I sensed He had other purposes in mind as well. Then, and in the many hours I've since contemplated that experience, many realizations and insights have come to mind. Allow me to pause briefly to share just a few of those insights before moving on with this testimony.

First, regarding spirits themselves: I had formerly assumed that the illustrations of spirits that one often encountered were, in essence, "artists' renditions." That is, like artists drawing illustrations of dinosaurs that disappeared eons ago, their depictions were based on considerable speculation. I realized now however that spirits have been and are observed by people and that many descriptions have come from first-hand experience. The spiritual realm is an indisputable reality that individuals have and do periodically witness. Spirits, at least human spirits, look exactly like the bodies they inhabit, except that spirits are translucent—very much like looking through fog, but with distinct shapes and edges. For example, our spirits were easily and immediately identifiable by our distinct outlines no matter which way we turned.

I then also realized that Jesus Himself continues to appear to people. In fact, many years before I became a Christian, a woman told me Jesus walked into her room one afternoon as she was vacuuming. She said they sat down together on the edge of her bed and He talked with her. I had believed her simple account at the time, but since I didn't know Christ nor believe in God, I wasn't certain who it really was that she thought was Jesus. Now I'm confident it *was* Jesus who spoke with her. I'm certain that many artists' paintings of Jesus find their inspiration in personal witness. I am positive she and I are not alone or unique among modern believers in having seen Jesus in this way.

I have often thought about that precise moment Jesus stepped into my Dad's living room. I knew instantly and without question that He was Jesus. He wasn't an angel. He wasn't some nameless ghost. He was Jesus — there was and could be no doubt. I think about how concrete that recognition was every time I read in Scripture passages of the spirits recognizing Jesus. Even though the crowds were confused and in disagreement about who He was, the spirits knew, instantly and without doubt. I now see more clearly that it is the action of the Holy Spirit working within us that opens our eyes and understanding to the presence of Jesus.

I mentioned that the thought "communion" kept coming to mind. I realized that the three of us were somehow in communion. While I still don't understand the entire meaning of that particular state of relationship, it seems at minimum to be a coming together in "oneness," a spiritual connection deeper than I'm able to fully grasp at this time. Although I don't fully understand it, it has given me a greater appreciation of the communion of saints, both those on earth and those already in heaven. It has given me a deeper appreciation of the Eucharist, or Holy Communion, believed by many Christians to be the true presence of Jesus under the appearance of bread and wine. It also has given me a deeper appreciation of the closeness Jesus desires. He has prayed, and it is truly His desire, that we be one with Him, as He is one with the Father (John 17:20, 21). Full communion with Him and the Father is Christ's sincere desire for each of us.

I should point out that preceding this miracle, and preceding every other profound miracle I've experienced, I had spent considerable time in prayer and in the Word, seeking God. Whenever I consistently pray and meditate on Scripture, I experience miracles. Why? God promises us in His Word, "You will seek me and find me, *when* (italics mine) you seek me with all your heart" (Jeremiah 29:13). We should expect nothing less. Yet that promise seems to hold a warning by inference: "Don't seek me, and you won't find me" it seems to imply. Truly, when I get unduly distracted by worldly affairs and am not faithful in prayer and Scripture reading, I seem to drift away from God. His power no longer seems to touch me in profound, experiential ways. I realize then that all that separates the holiest saints from the average Christian is that the saints actively and consistently seek God. They are "sold out for Jesus," so to speak. Holiness is a grace that God imparts to those who seek Him with all their heart.

Holiness comes *not* as a result of human willpower—but as a result of obedience, of giving God our hearts and our will. Only time spent with God makes us holy.

Finally, it also follows then that if we hope to find God's answers to our prayers, then we must place ourselves in communion with God. The outpouring of His grace to us requires an appropriate response on our part in order to assimilate that grace in our lives. Even then, we will still suffer pain and loss in our lives because we do live in a broken world. But in Christ Jesus, even amidst suffering and tragedy, God answers our prayer with the blessings of grace, courage, and peace—if we live in communal relationship with Him. Not even death itself can hold us, if we die in Christ.

"I AM WHO I AM," God declares (Exodus 3:14). He is Emmanuel, God among us. Today. Yesterday. Tomorrow. He is not simply an historical figure. He is not just some former person who will return in some distant future. He lives *now*. He is available to us *now*. He works among and within us *now*. We live in God's Kingdom *now*. The power, the grace, the joy, the peace, the love, the very essence of God's Kingdom, is available *now*. Why doesn't all humanity experience His Kingdom, His presence among us? Jesus explains it this way, "I am the way and the truth and the life. No one comes to the Father except through me" (John 14:6). It requires a radical acceptance of Jesus as Lord to open wide the door to God's Kingdom. "But seek first his kingdom and his righteousness, and all these things will be given to you as well" (Matthew 6:33). That is God's promise. That is what He delivers when we fervently seek and serve Him.

Going Home

Part of caring for my Dad required me to roll him onto one side, then the other, several times a day. I began to develop painful muscle spasms in my lower back from this effort. About three days after Christ's visit, the pain became severe. I called my brother, Jim, and asked if he could help. He readily agreed and drove over that afternoon.

That night I slept in the small spare guest room. Jim slept on the couch in the living room near Dad, where I had been sleeping all week. At precisely 5:00 a.m. an angel spoke to me. His exact words were "Your father just left." My eyes popped open at the sound of his voice but I could see no one in the room, yet I *knew* with clarity and absolute certainty that it had been an angel that had spoken. I got up, walked through the kitchen to the living room, and up to Dad's bed. As the angel had said, Dad was gone. His body lay still and lifeless on the hospital bed. Jim was awake, reading a book beneath the soft glow of the table light. I said, "Jim, Dad is gone." Jim looked up, noticing me for the first time. Then he replied, "Oh yeah...a couple of minutes ago his breathing became soft and peaceful. Then I started reading again and hadn't noticed it had stopped." Dad had gone home.

~

"'Do not let your hearts be troubled. Trust in God; trust also in me. In my Father's house are many rooms; if it were not so, I would have told you. I am going there to prepare a place for you. And if I go and prepare a place for you, I will come back and take you to be with me that you also may be where I am. You know the way to the place where I am going.'

Thomas said to him, 'Lord, we don't know where you are going, so how can we know the way?'

Jesus answered, 'I am the way and the truth and the life. No one comes to the Father except through me. If you really knew me, you would know my Father as well. From now on, you do know him and have seen him.'"

JOHN 14:1-7

Chapter Five

The Road to Catholicism

It happened at yet another *Promise Keepers* conference in the King-dome. Again, tens of thousands of men had gathered to worship God and to commit themselves to their Christian calling. This time I was attending with about twenty men I knew from a couple of Catholic churches in my area. We were seated in a group extending halfway across a section of seats. I was sitting on the inside edge of the group, and immediately to my right were men from other churches.

Once again this conference proved to be an amazing, life-chang-ing experience, as we praised and proclaimed Christ's glory, and were transformed by God's tangible presence. During a break the second day I started talking with one of the men on my right. In the course of conversation I asked him what church he attended. He said he attended a Christian and Missionary Alliance Church, one of the Evangelical Protestant denominations. In fact, he said he was the senior pastor there. What an amazing coincidence. I explained that I also attended a Christian and Missionary Alliance Church, Smokey Point Community Church in Marysville, WA. He knew the pastor and the various associate pastors who served there, so we talked about that church for a few minutes. Then I told him I also attended Immaculate Conception Church, a Catholic Church in Everett. The pastor looked puzzled and even concerned. So I explained that my wife was Catholic and that I attended the 8:30 a.m. service at Smokey Point, then picked her up for the 10 a.m. Mass at Immaculate. The pastor now looked somewhat distraught. How did that work, he asked, with her being Catholic and me obviously being Protestant? What about this Catholic idea of faith and works, he wondered out loud? I knew where he was going with this, but I also sensed that this was not the time for a theological debate. Instead of responding to his question directly, I motioned to the twenty men at my left and replied, "Pastor, I don't know about that. All I know is that these men love Jesus." Then in response to his questioning look I said, "Yes, they are all Catholic."

In that moment I watched God touch that pastor in a profound way, maybe more profoundly than he'd been touched in a while. You could see in his stunned expression that there was no doubt in his mind that these men loved Jesus, for they'd been worshiping passionately right beside the pastor all day. You could see him realizing that there was no way that they didn't enjoy the same personal, saving relationship with Jesus that he did. Yet they were Catholic. The reality of their obvious faith in Christ contrasted dramatically with what he thought he knew about Catholicism. What about this business of faith and works? Could Catholics be saved?

If you've been a Christian for very long you know what I'm talking about—one of the central theological disputes between Catholics and Protestants. In very simple terms, Protestants, (with somewhat varying positions depending on denomination) believe that you are saved by faith in Christ alone and that salvation is secured, not through our efforts, but through faith in Jesus Christ. Many believe that nothing else is required.

But Catholic teaching is more complex. Again in abbreviated terms, the Catholic Church teaches that attaining salvation is a process, not a one-time event, and that generally four conditions are central to that process. They are: believing in Jesus Christ as Lord and Savior (the same as Protestants); receiving Baptism (a sacramental work of Christ which "seals" us in Him and imparts within us His Holy Spirit); repenting of sin; and finally, intentionally following Christ in love and in obedience to Him. Catholics believe that for most people (with some exceptions depending on age and specific circumstances) all four are necessary elements of salvation.

Theologically the above two viewpoints seem irreconcilable. Since nothing in our existence is more important than our eternal fate, this has proved to be a volatile and divisive argument. In past centuries, Catholics labeled Protestants heretics and agents of Satan. Protestants returned the accusations. Coupled with emotion, ambition, politics, and the overall woundedness of our human condition, this dispute has sometimes erupted in intolerance, violence, and even wars. Both can't be correct, or can they? If one theology leads to heaven, then certainly the other must leave its followers short of heaven, destined for hell, right?

Although academically the two theologies appear at odds with one another, I would propose that in practice they both can produce the same result. Consider this. Suppose many Protestants are right. Suppose it is faith in Christ alone that secures our salvation. Are Catholics then going to hell because they believe other conditions must be met as well? No, not if it is truly only faith in Christ that secures our salvation. Why? Because Catholics who do acknowledge and follow Jesus Christ as their Lord do meet what these Protestants churches consider the only requirement for salvation. Any intellectual misunderstanding Catholics may have would be irrelevant if they otherwise meet that one indispensable condition: that is, to surrender their lives to Christ in faith.

But what if Catholics are correct? What if faith in Christ as Lord is not the whole picture? What if once we acknowledge Christ as Lord in our lives, we must respond to His commands; we must answer His call to live charitably toward one another? What if we need to repent of our sins and experience baptism for the forgiveness of sin? Would that mean that Protestants are going to hell? Certainly not. Why? Protestants (and the other Christian traditions that I'm aware of) also baptize and engage in charitable works. It is my own personal experience, and the experience of Christians for the past 2000 years, that once you make a decision to follow Christ and acknowledge Him as Lord in your life, He enters into your life in a tangible, life-transforming way. He changes you. I believe it is impossible for a person to truly accept Christ as their Lord and not be transformed. So what happens? The Methodists are out sharing Christ with their neighbors. The Baptists are feeding the poor in soup kitchens. The Greek Orthodox are donating money to the missionaries who come to their church. The Lutherans are supporting orphanages in Russia. They all baptize in the name of the Father, Son, and Holy Spirit. Are they trying to work their way to heaven? Are they trying to gain salvation through ritual? No, they are simply answering God's call in their lives. They are living like Christ is King in their lives, because they have invited Him and allowed Him to be the King in their lives. That is exactly what Catholics are talking about. So if Catholic theology is correct, then believing Protestants are certainly bound for heaven as well.

For me, Protestant salvation theology poignantly emphasizes the essential substance of our reconciliation with God—a personal relationship with Jesus Christ. Catholic salvation theology most precisely portrays for me what that saving relationship looks like—the complete surrendering of one's life to Jesus Christ; two sides of the same coin. From almost the beginning of my conversion I recognized that we are one Body in Christ: Catholics, Protestants, Orthodox, Anglican, Messianic Jews, even in spite of our theological differences.

So it wasn't theology that led me to the Catholic Church, not that we shouldn't seek sound theology. Instead, it was another God experience that brought me here.

It happened on Father Dennis Robb's 25th anniversary as a priest. Our parishes hosted a gathering to celebrate the event. The celebration took place at the Everett Yacht Club, which houses a large banquet hall at water's edge overlooking Port Gardner Bay. The dining facility is designed to seat approximately 200 people. My wife and I arrived a little late. We were both stunned as we entered the large hall.

Spread out before us was an immense crowd of smiling faces. The room was absolutely packed; literally standing room only. Every conceivable space was filled with people chatting, smiling, and laughing. I was struck by two facts. First, a great love permeated that room. People's faces beamed with joy. Laughter filled the air. Secondly, I realized that I recognized most of the people present, at least by face if not by name. They were people I worshiped beside every week in church, or served on commissions with, or sat with at our kids' basketball games. I felt a great affection for all of them, and an intimate connection to each of them.

Then God spoke to me in a clear, unmistakable voice. He said, "Bill, look at the family I gave you. Aren't they wonderful?"

"Yes Lord," I answered, "they certainly are." At that moment I knew I was called to join the Catholic Church. God had spoken.

So in September of 1999, I enrolled in *The Rite of Christian Initiation for Adults (RCIA),* a program that prepares people to enter fully into the sacramental life of the Catholic Church. I entered RCIA expecting it to be primarily an educational experience; simply required knowledge about Catholicism before receiving Confirmation. In fact we did learn a great deal about the Mass and the central doctrines of the Church. However, RCIA proved to be much more than educational. It proved to be what the Church intends it to be: formative. Through the faith, the shared experiences, and the love of the instructors, sponsors, and other catechumens, we were drawn by the Holy Spirit into a remarkable experience of unity, and drawn into a deeper, more intimate relationship with Christ. It was a powerful faith building experience, because it was a powerful tangible experience of Christ active among us and within us. For some it proved to be a path to their first personal tangible encounter with Christ.

This was demonstrated most succinctly during our last week of preparation before being confirmed. One of the sponsors stood up and stated that she had asked the woman whom she had sponsored to say a few words. Then, with her encouragement, the young lady sitting beside her stood up. She was a person who had not said much during our many discussions over the past months. Yet now, in a quiet voice, this polite young woman told her story. She was originally from Japan, she began in a soft accent. She had met and married her husband, a serviceman at the time, when he was stationed in Japan a few years before. They were now parents to young children. Although she was raised in an eastern religion in Japan, her husband strongly encouraged her to become Catholic. Dutifully she consented, signing up for RCIA, but secretly intending to join the Church in name only. Then something entirely unexpected happened. Through RCIA she came to experience and know Jesus personally. She shared how He had come into her life, how she came to know Him as her Lord and Savior. She shared how Jesus had revealed His love to her and of her joy in His promise of Heaven. She shared how she had surrendered her life to

Him and how she could never again live without Him. Like hundreds of millions of souls before her, she testified to the reality, the presence, the intimacy, the love and the power of Jesus Christ in her life.

A week later, on Easter Vigil, in the year 2000, she, I, and dozens of others, made our profession of faith at Immaculate Conception Church in Everett, WA. We received the Sacraments of Confirmation, Eucharist, and for those who had not previously been baptized in a Christian church, Baptism. Father Dennis Robb, the inspiring priest who several years earlier had first given me a glimpse of the great promise of Christianity, anointed me with oil, laid hands on me, and prayed that I receive God's Spirit of holiness (Isaiah 11:2-3). *I had come home.*

(One day all of us who belong to Christ will stand at the gates of heaven. Spread before us will be a sea of faces—a great body of saints who in their earthly lives followed Christ as Presbyterians or Messianic Jews, as United Church of Christ or Episcopalians, as Lutherans, Baptists, Pentecostals, or Catholics, or in non-denominational Christian community churches throughout the world. There Jesus will stand with us, looking out over the great multitudes. He will say, "Look at the family I gave you. Aren't they wonderful?" And we will all know we have come home).

‿

"The body is a unit, though it is made up of
many parts; and though all its parts are many,
they form one body. So it is with Christ. For we
were all baptized by one Spirit into one body—
whether Jews or Greeks, slave or free—and
we were all given the one Spirit to drink."

1 CORINTHIANS 12:12-13

45

Epilogue

To my Christian Friends

I pray confidently that this testimony has been an encouragement to you, my brothers and sisters in Christ. Some of the experiences related in this testimony may seem more dramatic than your own, while some of you have experienced God in ways and situations far more dramatic than those described here. Yet it is not *how* we experience God that is the miracle, but that we experience God *at all*. For as the psalmist observed, "What is man that you (God) should be mindful of him?" (Psalm 8:4). We don't deserve such grace. Yet over and over, in ways ranging from subtle to dramatic, the God and Creator of the universe interacts and reveals Himself to those who earnestly seek Him.

There may be some reading this testimony who are thinking to themselves, "I believe in God. I believe Jesus died for our sins, but I can't honestly say I *know* Him in the sense this guy's talking about. I'm not aware of any tangible presence or divine power in my life. What can I do to experience God in a fuller way?"

I suggest that the first and most critical step is to examine what kind of relationship you've chosen to have with Christ. Are you allowing Christ to be master of your life, or are you retaining control? Have you invited Jesus to be Savior *and* Lord in your life? Or, in examining your priorities and the choices you make, would it be more accurate to say you've decided that you'll stay Lord and He can be Savior. The truth is we either accept Him as *both* Savior *and* Lord, or we risk experiencing Him as neither. Until we make that conscious decision to follow Christ with all we have, no matter the cost, and no matter where He leads us, we choke out the grace He desires to pour into our lives. To experience the power of God *in* our lives, we have to consciously yield power *over* our lives to Him. That can be difficult for many of us. Following Christ is a radical decision. But if we're willing to *try* to surrender to His authority, Jesus will infuse grace into our efforts and supply what we can't. Submitting our will to Christ is the first, and unavoidable, step.

Also, we should maintain an attitude of confident hopefulness as we seek a deeper relationship with God. Approach Jesus with expectant faith. Christ wants to help us. Even more than we desire an intimate, personal relation with Him, He desires that relationship with us. Just as Jesus is one with the Father, so too has He prayed that we would be one with Him (John 17:21). He will bring us into that tangible personal experience as we open our hearts more fully to Him. He will supply in us what we lack, and accomplish in us what we could never do through willpower alone.

So in what ways can we open our hearts more fully to Christ? One essential way is that we spend significant time with Him; good, quality time. That is the second unavoidable response on our part. Spending just an hour a week in church with the Lord is not enough time to develop a powerful personal relationship. We need daily interaction. And daily personal prayer is the foundation of this interaction. Set aside a time each day to listen to the Lord, to thank Him, to praise Him, to sit quietly just being with Him, to bring your needs and concerns before Him.

Be mindful also that the Lord dwells within you in the person of the Holy Spirit (1 Corinthians 6:19). That means you don't occupy your body alone. You have a roommate, God Himself. Be attentive to your roommate throughout the day. Ask Jesus to increase your capacity to recognize the prompting of His Spirit, and then respond to the Spirit when He nudges you. Seek His presence and His guidance in your daily activities.

Seek God every day in the Bible, His Word. Daily reading of the Bible will transform you supernaturally. It will enlighten you, empower you, heal you, infuse you with wisdom and understanding, sustain you, and reveal to you the heart and person of God. "For the word of God is living and active. Sharper than any double-edged sword, it penetrates even to dividing soul and spirit, joints and marrow; it judges the thoughts and attitudes of the heart" (Hebrews 4:12). The Bible is not a book *about* God. It is God's *living communication* to you.

Connecting with the Church is essential to strengthening our relationship with Jesus. We are a family, the children of God, the Body of Christ, with Christ as our head. A relationship with Jesus is not something we can nurture in a vacuum. God desires a personal relationship with each of us, yes, but not an exclusive relationship with any one of us. We need to be connected to one another to experience the fullness of God's power in our lives. One of the key ways that God touches us and nourishes us is through other Christians.

Sin is a serious obstacle to a healthy, vibrant relationship with God. Perform an examination of conscience on a regular basis. Do you love God and others as Jesus Himself commands us to love? (See John 13:34). Do you remember the Ten Commandments? (See Exodus 20:1-17). Be honest with yourself. Do you fervently seek to obey God's commandments, or do you pick and choose which commandments you'll obey? If we truly desire that Christ be King in our lives, then we do the things He commands us to do and avoid that which He commands us not to do. If, on the other hand, we pick and choose which commandments we'll follow, then in reality we are appointing ourselves king, and relegating Christ to some lesser position. We cannot experience the power of Christ *in* our lives, unless we submit power *over* our lives to Him. Turn away from sin.

Do you struggle with obedience to God? We all do. Do you experience periods where you lack an appropriate awe for God, when even your love for God seems to dwindle? We all do. But here's the good news. Jesus Himself will bring us back in awe before the holiness and majesty of God, if we turn to Him with all our heart. How many of us are willing to trust Jesus for our salvation, yet when it comes to sanctification, our attitude seems to be "We'll take it from here"? We attempt to overcome temptations, addictions, and character issues through willpower alone. That invariably fails, and it often leads to guilt, frustration, and a pulling away from God. Instead, trust Jesus for holiness, as well as your salvation. Take your struggles to Him in prayer and in reconciliation, asking Him and trusting Him to heal you of your weaknesses, and He will transform and empower you to overcome those obstacles to holiness. Wait on the Lord with patience and expectant faith.

Growing in holiness is *not* a matter of exercising exceptional willpower or of overcoming temptation by our own human strength. Instead, it is a matter of first inviting, and then allowing, the One who is holy to take over our thoughts and lives. It is a matter of us becoming less, so that He can become more. It is a matter of yielding our will to the divine will of the Holy Spirit who dwells within us. It is a radical, uncompromising submission to Christ. Make that decision and Christ

Himself will change everything. You don't have to do it yourself (and couldn't anyway by your own power). The more time we spend with Christ in communion, in prayer, in worship, in the Word, and in active obedience, the more we grow in our capacity to allow His Spirit to operate freely within us and the more we grow in holiness and in personal awareness of His presence in our life.

Conversion then, is a process, a lifelong experience of growing in closer union with Christ as we seek to more fully surrender our lives to Him. My observation over the past few years is that this coming to *know* God, this conversion process, seems to work itself out in three general forms. One form is represented by my own experience: a nonbeliever surrenders to Christ and is then transformed in supernaturally infused faith; growing in knowledge and understanding as he or she continues to follow Christ within the Church. This is an extremely dramatic, night versus day sort of conversion. It is a very tangible "born again" experience. It is a very visible first step in this journey with the Lord.

A second form of conversion I've witnessed involves people who, for one reason or another (usually because they were raised in a Christian environment), had considered themselves Christian, but had never tangibly experienced Christ personally—perhaps had never truly, unconditionally, surrendered their lives to Christ. Then at some point in their journey they felt called to make a deeper commitment. Maybe a tragedy prompted the decision or maybe they were moved by a word of encouragement from someone. In any event, in that fertile field of obedience, Christ revealed Himself in a tangible way. The individual experienced what might be described as an "awakening" of faith. That awakening is also a born again experience.

Finally, I've known Christians who would say they've just always believed. They do in fact know and tangibly experience God in their lives. These people were most often raised Christian from early childhood. As they grew and matured, they gradually and almost unconsciously surrendered their lives to Christ. Jesus himself became a tangible part of their lived experience. The Catholic Church describes this process of conversion as "formation." Although born again in Baptism and in lived faith, these people often have trouble relating to that terminology, because the transformation was so gradual and began so early in their lives.

While I pray that this testimony would bless you, my fellow Christians, I confess it was not written primarily with you in mind. Instead I wrote it for those who probably would never come across it on their own—for non-Christians. Why for non-Christians? Because there exists a truth related to Christian faith that only personal testimony can adequately convey. You already know it. Non-Christians deserve to hear it.

That truth is simply this: faith in God comes from a tangible, lived experience of God. We believe in God because we *know* God. That is a truth that non-Christians are literally dying to hear. I implore you to share your own personal experience of God with others. I invite you to share this testimony with them as well.

To my Non-Christian Friends

Now to those of you who are not yet believers, who are reading this testimony because someone who cares about you has encouraged you to do so—I'd like to offer a personal message.

First, thank you for allowing me to share my experiences with you through this testimony. Please know that every experience I've shared is absolutely true and that these experiences are not unique. Untold millions of Christians have encountered Christ in similar ways around the world and throughout the centuries.

I remember as a former non-believer myself that it would baffle me no end when Christians would ask me if I "knew" Jesus. I assumed, as perhaps you might, that their "faith" was the result of their own intellectual conclusions, and that any imagined knowledge they claimed was simply faulty analysis on their part. Yet, I've come to experience conclusively myself that Christian faith is not the same kind of faith most of us typically refer to when we say we *believe* something. We may *believe* the Yankees will make it to the World Series or not. We may *believe* the current President is a hero or a scoundrel. We may *believe* in a principle, cause, or nation so entirely that we are willing to risk our lives for it; yet that is not the same kind of faith that the Bible refers to when it speaks of faith. The above examples actually only represent strong personal opinions on our part, do they not? These opinions, or *beliefs*, are all arrived at through our own reasoning process. They are the result of a work, an intellectual work that we all participate in. This kind of faith is what I previously assumed Christians were talking about when they said they believed in Jesus. Since through my own intellectual analysis I had reached a different conclusion, I often assumed Christians were naïve, irrational, or perhaps even less than bright.

Yet the Bible teaches that faith comes not from our own works, but that rather it is a divine gift from God (Ephesians 2:8). Faith is a gift, a work of the Holy Spirit who dwells within us, imparted to us by the Spirit. It is a gift that God offers to each of us personally, but which we can only receive if we are willing to receive the One who sends it. When we invite Jesus to come as Lord into our lives, God Himself takes up residence within us, in the person of the Holy Spirit. His Spirit witnesses to our spirit. Divine belief in God is to *know* God through unmistakable personal experience of God. God is a real, tangible, identifiable, living Person - not a product of people's analysis, imagination, opinions, or conclusions.

I've tried to keep this book short, yet offer enough examples to demonstrate the simple truth reiterated throughout this testimony. *You can know God.* Not just know about Him. Not just accept Him or reject Him based on the strengths or weaknesses of your analytical abilities. But you can actually *know* Him: *know* His vibrant, unmistakable presence in your life; *know* His love for you personally; *know* that salvation is available to you, that an eternal home is being prepared for you in heaven; *know* God without doubt or reservation. Again, faith is a grace given by God, not a work of the human intellect. You are only called to choose Christ first. You risk nothing by making this decision. I encourage you to make that decision now.

Some people want Christ, but somehow don't feel worthy. They're right; they're not worthy. Nor are you. Nor am I. Whatever virtue we possess of our own volition pales in comparison to the holiness of God. We all fall short of the perfection to which He calls us, and for which we were created. But isn't that the point? If we could be "good enough" through our own efforts to maintain a vibrant, personal relationship with God, Christ need not have sacrificed Himself on the cross as atonement for our sin. The hard truth is, we cannot stand before God aside from Christ—God is infinitely beyond us in holiness and purity, and is wounded grievously by any sin. Yet no matter our past, we have never been bad enough to be rejected by Christ. He is eager to forgive past mistakes if we would but repent and submit our lives to Him now. He strengthens us in our struggle against temptation and dysfunctional patterns of behavior. He cleans up areas of our lives we aren't even aware need cleaning up. He offers himself as atonement for that which we can't conquer on our own. He forgives all that we repent of. Nothing you have ever done can separate you from the love of Christ. When you stand before God in Christ, our Father promises that your sins will have been removed from you "as far as east is from the west" (Psalm 103: 12), as if you had never sinned. That is the hope and promise of salvation that Christ extends to you even at this very moment. I invite and encourage you to accept His salvation now—to surrender your life to Christ and to invite Him to be Lord and Savior in your life. Please, open your heart to Him now and He will transform your life.

A word of advice from my own experience: when you do choose Christ, connect with the body of Christian believers as soon as possible. Particularly seek out and connect with small faith-sharing groups within the larger body, such as Bible study groups, prayer groups, worship groups, etc. Find mature Christians to mentor you. I cannot overemphasize the importance of Christian fellowship. When you accept Christ, you step into the front lines of a spiritual battle, the intensity and pervasiveness of which would be difficult for you to comprehend at this time. We need the support of other Christians for our faith to survive and grow. We need their prayerful protection and the benefit of their experience and wisdom. We need the Word of God and the divinely appointed ministry of the Church. Additionally, through the mentoring of mature Christians, God will prepare you for whatever specific mission He has in mind for you personally. Jesus calls us to be His body; His hands on earth. He calls us not only for our own sake, but for the sake of others that He would touch through us. Christianity is not a spectator sport; it is a family affair. God each of us a job to do.

One word of caution: although the Church preaches torically recognized and theologically accurate divine natu Christ (that Christ is *eternally one in being with God th* aware that in the past century or so there have appeare handful of splinter denominations that represent ther tian, but that have developed theologies far remov

Christian understanding and long historic experience. A small handful of denominations incorrectly present Jesus as a created being; perhaps an anointed teacher or prophet sent by God for a specific purpose, but still just a man. One group even proposes that Jesus was created originally as a man, but then later evolved into a god, and that even men today have an opportunity to evolve to a similar status and create their own universes in some distant future. Another view holds that all world visions of God are equally valid, that it doesn't really matter who you worship as God. Jesus, Buddha, a golden calf—they're all the same to them. These diluted representations of the nature of Jesus fall far short of the fullness of the promise and the power of Christ. Connect instead with those who accept Jesus Christ as Lord and Savior, as God among us, as eternally one in being with the Father and with the Holy Spirit. The Apostle Thomas expressed the reality of Christ's nature most succinctly 2000 years ago when, upon placing his fingers in the nail holes and punctured side of the risen Jesus, proclaimed "My Lord and my God!" (John 20:28). This is the Jesus we proclaim in Christianity. This is the Jesus who will transform your life and bring you to the fullness of eternal life with the Father. This is the Jesus proclaimed in the Catholic Church since its founding 2000 years ago when Christ first commissioned the Apostle Peter to be the rock upon which He would build His Church; in the Eastern Church since its split with the Roman Church almost 1000 years ago; in the Anglican Church since its separation from Rome five centuries ago, and in the vast majority of the Protestant denominations that grew out of the Reformation over the past 500 years. We all continue to recognize and experience the divine nature and eternally infinite power of Jesus Christ, as we submit our lives to Him. This is the Body of Christ to which I invite you.

Finally, let me say that I am tremendously excited for all that God has in store for you in Christ Jesus. God bless you richly in your walk with Him. Allow me to close by praying our Lord's own heart for you, as expressed through St. Paul in his prayer for the Ephesians:

"For this reason I kneel before the Father, from whom his whole family in heaven and on earth derives its name. I pray that out of his glorious riches he may strengthen you with power through his Spirit in your inner being, so that Christ may dwell in your hearts through faith. And I pray that you, being rooted and established in love, may have power, together with all the saints, to grasp how wide and long and high and deep is the love of Christ, and to know this love that surpasses knowledge, that you may be filled to the measure of all the fullness of God.

Now to him who is able to do immeasurably more than all we ask or imagine, according to his power that is at work within us, to him be glory in the church and in Christ Jesus throughout all generations, for ever and ever! Amen."

EPHESIANS 3:14-21

Bill Odell
Ellensburg, WA

Addendum

Frequently Asked Questions

Near the beginning of this testimony I mentioned a few of the seemingly insurmountable questions I had previously entertained regarding foundational Christian tenets. Since I've become a Christian I've had many non-believers ask me the same or similar questions. Following is how I might answer some of those questions:

If God does love us, and is absolutely all-powerful, how can He allow such suffering to go on in the world? Why doesn't He just use His power to fix us all so we won't keep hurting ourselves and each other?

God intentionally created us with free will; with the ability and the freedom to choose between right and wrong. I'll explain why:

God created us out of love, like a Father, to become a family who loves Him in return. In fact, it is difficult to understand God outside the context of family. He created us to be His children. True, He could have created us to be like robots, programmed to "love" Him and each other unfailingly. But "love" that is not freely chosen is not really love at all. It's just a pre-programmed, robotic response. So God created us in His image, gracing us with free will, in order that we might *choose* to love Him and each other and thus become the real family He desires us to be. He longs for children, not robots.

Tragically, throughout the history of mankind, many have frequently chosen not to love God or each other. Our tendency toward selfishness, greed, envy, pride, lack of forgiveness, anger and violence (in a word, sin) has been passed on from generation to generation, with widely destructive influences on all of mankind. The world's frequent rejection of God, who is the source of life and all that is good, has resulted in a brokenness and chaos that ripples throughout all humanity. Consequently, dysfunction, conflict, suffering, and death now define our human condition. Thus, even relatively good people are touched by suffering; not because they deserve it, but because the accumulative, destructive effect of a broken humanity touches us all.

To "fix" us as individuals and to fix humanity as a whole, God would have to take away our free will, and thus also our status as children of God. Without free will, we would more resemble automated machines in God's garden, rather than the loving children He desires and intends us to be. God has a much higher destiny in mind for us than to be mere robots; a much higher hope for us than we often have for ourselves.

Christians claim they believe in one God, yet profess that God exists in three Persons. How can that be?

Consider the common egg. An egg is comprised of an egg yolk, an egg white, and a shell. Three distinct components, yet still a single egg.

This analogy from the natural world has some theological weak points, but it does at least give us a framework from which to formulate some sort of mental picture of the Trinity (Three Divine Persons in One God). The truth is that creation can never, in and of itself, adequately define the Creator.

Consider God for a moment. This Being is so immense in power that at His command all of creation has come into existence. This Being has always existed, and will always exist. This Being exists in all places simultaneously, and in all time simultaneously. This Being set in motion all the laws of nature, yet is subject to none of them. This Being is the source of everything we can see, feel, smell, hear, or measure, even with the most sophisticated scientific equipment. Yet this Being cannot in turn be measured by either our physical senses or our scientific equipment. We live in a "box" (the sum total of all that is) which God created. Yet God exists apart from, outside of, before and after this "box".

So can you call forth a clear mental image of God yet? Me neither. God is *way* beyond anything of this world. Yet our minds are dependent on this world for the points of reference from which our intellect formulates conceptions. Thus any mental picture of the Trinity we might devise for ourselves will always fall short.

Yet from the earliest days of the Church, Christians recognized the triune nature of God. Through the inspired writers of the Bible, God refers to Himself in the singular over 4000 times. He is *One* God. Yet the Bible also refers to God as the Father (over 250 times) as the Son (over 140 times) and as the Holy Spirit (over 320 times). Not three separate "gods" in one Person, mind you, but Three Divine Persons in One God; God in Himself. So while our intellect is unable to articulate a definitive picture of God, His Spirit witnesses to us on the spiritual level. Jesus said, "...no one knows the Father except the Son and those to whom the Son chooses to reveal him" (Matthew 11:27). It is through a relationship with Jesus that our spirit is opened to the reality of God, and our spiritual eyes to the Three Divine Persons in One God; God the Father, God the Redeemer, and God the Transforming Presence: Father, Son, and Holy Spirit.

How could God allow His own Son to be tortured and killed? Why did Jesus have to die?

Sin cannot abide in the glorious eternal presence of God, who is holy beyond human comprehension. So Jesus offered Himself as a ransom for the deliverance of mankind from our sin, and from the fate our sinful acts had earned us, namely eternal separation from God. "For the wages of sin is death, but the gift of God is eternal life in Christ Jesus our Lord" (Romans 6:23). Jesus, who was without sin, took our sin upon Himself and died in our place, freeing us from the bondage of sin. He paid the price we couldn't.

But we have to wonder, couldn't God have chosen another way to redeem us, short of sacrificing His own divine Son? I expect the answer to that is yes. So maybe the more appropriate question is:

Why did God choose the suffering, death, and resurrection of Jesus as *the most suitable way* to redeem mankind and restore our relationship with Him?

To answer that question, let us consider some ways in which Jesus' death and resurrection were particularly suitable for bringing about the repentance and deliverance of mankind.

Jesus (God incarnate) came in the flesh to mankind at a time when the cultures of the day believed that only the shedding of blood could atone for sin. God himself had instructed the Israelites in careful detail in the offering of sacrifice—the blood representing life, and the sacrifice representing the surrendering of one's own life to God. So by offering himself as a blood sacrifice, Jesus modeled for the people of His time, in a way they could readily comprehend, that He was truly the path to a restored relationship with God. His sacrifice connected intellectually, emotionally and theologically with the people of that age; drawing people to Himself, and through Him, to the Father. The early Christians would have readily recognized and accepted Jesus, the Son of God, as the logical and perfect sacrifice for forgiveness and redemption.

But most particularly, Jesus' death was a most suitable means for our deliverance for this reason: unless He died, He could not rise. It was the resurrection of the Christ that changed human history for all time. The widely witnessed and widely proclaimed resurrection of Jesus, following His very public and much publicized death on the cross, rocked mankind to its core. His resurrection confirmed His claim of divinity, and modeled God's promise of an afterlife, not only to the people of that age, but to people of all ages. Jesus' resurrection stands as a vivid and powerful testimony to the authenticity of God's promise of eternal life, and testifies to the immensity of God's work on our behalf. Death cannot hold us.

Jesus' death on the cross also speaks to the extraordinary lengths to which God is willing to go in order to save us from ourselves; to draw us back to Him. That God was willing to sacrifice his own Son to pay the penalty we owe for our transgressions speaks to His unconditional love for you and me. To this day the image of the crucifix stands as a powerful symbol of the immensity of God's love for mankind, drawing us to repentance, and evoking from us a sincere love for Him in response to His unconditional love for us. For while we were still sinners, Christ died for us (Romans 5:8).

You and I see suffering from an earthly perspective which is constrained by our human limitations. God sees suffering from an eternal perspective, unlimited because He is God. We typically view any suffering as bad. But God recognizes that in some circumstances suffering can be redemptive in nature, helping us and others grow closer to Him and to eternal life in heaven. And while suffering is temporary, the wage of unrepented sin is eternal; so suffering that frees us from sin is, in the context of our eternal fate, beneficial. Jesus' death on the cross stands as a vivid example of redemptive suffering.

Jesus' death was also redemptive in a supernatural sense. See the answer to the following question.

How could Jesus' death on the cross restore man's relationship with God?

When Jesus' disciples attempted to dissuade Him from submitting to execution, Jesus answered, "Unless I go away, the Counselor [the Holy Spirit] will not come to you; but if I go, I will send him to you" (John 16:7). Upon returning to the Father, following His death and resurrection, Jesus sent the Holy Spirit (the Spirit who proceeds from the Father and the Son) to dwell within those who accepted and believed in Him. The Holy Spirit, on a spiritual, supernatural level, expresses God's holiness through us, and cleanses us from the life-robbing effects of sin. It is the indwelling action of the Holy Spirit that reveals to us our errors, strengthens us, witnesses to us of the reality and the presence of God, and empowers us to battle temptation and strive to live in obedience to God. The Holy Spirit transforms us and makes us sharers in the divine life of God.

I'm a pretty good person. Why do I need atonement for my "sins"? Why can't God just accept me the way I am?

Pretty good compared to what? If I'm measuring myself against the rest of mankind, I've chosen a pretty low standard, wouldn't you say? Just because I don't cheat on my spouse, beat my kids, or lie on my tax return, doesn't necessarily mean I'm all that great. When we compare ourselves to the inexpressible holiness of God, who is absolutely perfect, and realize that we were created to be his children, perfect as He is perfect (a little lower than the angels, He tells us, crowned with glory and honor (Hebrews 2:7)), then suddenly we don't look all that hot. The sad truth is our sinful tendencies are passed from each generation to the next. They are unavoidable. Truthfully, being a good person is a far cry from being a perfect person. Yet everyone in heaven will be perfect.

God loves each of us, even in spite of our sin. But God, who is perfect, is grievously wounded by sin. God is so perfect that no sin can abide in His eternal presence. That's why you and I need to be cleansed of our sin and healed of our tendency toward sin before we can stand for all eternity before the holiness of God. And Jesus comes to us to do just that. He comes to us and accepts us just as we are right now, imperfections and all. Jesus then draws us into Himself, into His Holiness, transforming us into a new creation (2 Corinthians 5:17), and after we leave this earthly life, presents us before the Father without blemish, transformed for all eternity.

I sometimes hear Christians claim that their particular denomination teaches the *authentic* Gospel, sometimes even asserting that Christians from some other denominations won't go to heaven because of their theological misunderstandings. So even if I did decide to accept and follow Christ, how would I know which church to join?

I heard a preacher mention one time that he had just returned from a guided fishing trip somewhere in the south. He said that he noticed on that trip that the guides didn't clean the fish until after they caught them. My point being that we should put first things first. Choose Jesus first and submit your life to Him. Then having been "caught" by Christ, you will have Him to help guide you to the particular church where you need to be. It may not be the first church you try, but as you draw closer and closer to Christ, your discernment will develop ever more fully. If you are seeking Christ earnestly but do happen to land in a church with some questionable theological positions or one that expresses a somewhat distorted worldly view rather than a Godly view, you will come to recognize it in time. It is not the name over the door of the church you attend that assures your salvation; it is the nature of the relationship you have with Jesus Christ.

If God really does love us, how could He send some of us to Hell?

He doesn't. We choose hell. We have free will.

God is love, the source of everything good. If we refuse to allow God into this life on earth, by default we end up with what is left when we die, which is everything except that which is good - anguish, crushing hopelessness, consuming terror, an eternity separated from God; in a word, hell. We have been given free will now, in this lifetime, to choose. In the afterlife, however, we live eternally by the choice we make now. God clearly offers us the means to reconciliation and eternal life through Jesus Christ. He clearly warns us of what's at stake, and the consequences of rejecting His offer. If we end up in hell, I promise you, God is not the one we'll blame.

There are many non-Christian religions in the world that seek God, and profess to have insight into His nature. Are their followers going to hell just because they happened to be raised in the "wrong" religion?

Although the Gospel offers no clear path to heaven except through Jesus, many Christians, meditating on the love and mercy of the Father as revealed by the Person of Jesus Christ, expect that God does have some plan in place for those of non-Christian religions who earnestly seek to know and obey Him. Still, Jesus proclaimed in no uncertain terms, "I am the way and the truth and the life. No one comes to the Father except through me" (John 14:6). That message is reiterated and restated in dozens of different ways throughout the New Testament. The Bible describes Jesus as the Author of Life, the Author and Perfecter of our faith, and in fact the "one mediator between God and men." (1 Timothy 2:5)

Why is the intervention of Jesus so critical to our salvation? It's not because His sacrifice on the cross provided some sort of "symbolic" atonement for our sins. None of us leave this life on earth sinless, or completely free of our penchant to sin. Yet no one steps into heaven carrying sin, or any tendency to sin. The inhabitants of heaven are absolutely free of jealousy, envy, pride, anger, resentment, cruelty (intended or accidental), malice, dishonesty, low self-esteem, inflated self-esteem, disobedience, indifference toward God and one another, and a thousand other characteristics that distinguish our fallen human nature from the perfect holiness of our Creator. Something happens between that moment we leave this body behind, and the moment we step into heaven. And that something takes place on the spiritual level. We need a guide to lead us through the spiritual realm. We need a sinless witness to proclaim us worthy before God. And we need a supernatural transformation from our sinful self to the new creation we're to be in heaven. Jesus effects all of that for us on our behalf, if we submit our lives to Him.

So all I can say is that I hope God has a plan for bringing sincere individuals of all religions into His eternal kingdom. I just don't know what that plan might be. Christ is the only way I know *for sure* to get to heaven. For that reason, I will never stop proclaiming salvation through Jesus Christ.

I hear people talk about God's wrath. He sounds vindictive to me. Is God on an ego trip?

No, God is neither egotistical nor vindictive. His commands are not for His benefit, but for ours. He corrects us to keep us from destroying ourselves. The stakes are huge, and the consequences *are* eternal. To what extent would you go to dissuade your young children from playing on the freeway? Would you punish them in some way if it could serve to save their lives in the long run? God's concern for us is even greater, the consequences of our disobedience far deadlier, and His desperation for our salvation unfathomable. "But God demonstrates his own love for us in this: While we were still sinners, Christ died for us" (Romans 5:8). God is not vindictive. He has proven Himself unimaginably loving and merciful. Just look at the cross; at the price He was willing to pay out of love on our behalf.

I tried church for a while, but couldn't stand the phony pretense of some people there. How do you put up with the hypocrites?

I love them. That's what Jesus does.

Remember, none of us are perfect yet; we're all on a journey. Moreover, aside from a direct revelation from God, we can't see into other people's hearts. Is that person (whom you know to have cheated on both his wife and his tax returns outside of church) acting all holy in church just to disguise his many transgressions? Or does he appear pious and holy in church because he's taken a couple of hours away from his own worldly brokenness to focus on God, and is being touched by the transforming presence of the Almighty? The more fouled up we are, the more important it is that we get connected to the divine Healer. I want the hypocrites in Church. In every message we hear, every worship song we sing, every instance where we partake of the cup, lies the potential for God to reach us, change us, and heal us.

A perfect church would be nice though. I tell people that if they find a perfect church to let me know and I'll join it. I just forewarn them that once I join it, it won't be perfect anymore.

I can think of many times when God didn't answer my prayers. Since He supposedly loves us and is all powerful, how do you explain unanswered prayers?

I have personally witnessed countless answered prayers in my life and in the lives of other Christians.

Yet it is true that we've all prayed for things we thought God ought to do for us, but then didn't see the answer we'd hoped for. What is that about? Some Christians would say that God doesn't always gives us exactly what we ask for, but that He does give us what we need most. That is certainly quite often true, and often evident when we look closely. But what about those inexplicable tragedies that make no sense at all? What can we say to a mother who has just lost her child to accident, disease, or violence? Where was God's answer to her prayers?

Sometimes it is just not evident how God could possibly be working all things together for the good when we encounter senseless tragedy or relentless struggle in our lives. The truth is we live in a relationship with God and with one another that is far too complex for the human intellect to penetrate. Be mindful that while God is at work in our lives, so too is our own free will, as well as the free will of others, the influence of spiritual forces, and the accumulated effect of the sinful acts of all mankind. Sometimes tragedy strikes and we can find no rational answer.

The hard truth is we live in a broken world; broken by mankind's frequent rejection of God and His precepts. In the act of closing the door on God, man inadvertently (but sometimes intentionally) opened the door to Satan's destructive influence. Hence death, illness, violence and every sort of affliction entered into the human condition. This was not God's choosing, but the result of mankind's choices. Thus, we will all die one day. We will all experience suffering in this life. Prayer clearly doesn't always change the course of events according to our desires (although it often does). But prayer can always change our response to the course of events and how those events impact the rest of our lives.

The beautiful truth is that God loves us unconditionally and desires the best for us. Jesus announced that He came that we "may have life, and have it to the full" (John 10:10). Yet even Jesus, the Son of God, endured persecution, abandonment, and a horribly violent and torturous death. Although free of all sin Himself, Jesus entered into a world already badly broken, so in spite of His absolute innocence, He too experienced suffering. We Christians can't expect to escape all suffering in this life. But we can expect and trust that God, through prayer, can and will free us from much unnecessary suffering, and give us the strength and courage to carry us through the suffering that does enter our lives. There is incomparable peace in knowing God's presence even in the midst of our greatest struggles; in knowing that God is leading us to an eternal life with Him—free finally and forever of all suffering.

Now a word about answered prayer. Jesus said "You may ask for anything in my name, and I will do it" (John 14:14). Some misconstrue that promise to mean that all we have to do is drop the name "Jesus" and our prayer will be answered. But God is not some miracle vending machine in the sky in which we can insert a coin with the word "Jesus" imprinted on it, pull the lever, and expect our miracle to pop out. And frankly, neither are our prayers effective in changing God in any way. Instead, the reason we are encouraged to pray unceasingly is because our prayers open our hearts to God so that He can change and ultimately heal us. When the Bible speaks of "the name of Jesus" it is not just identifying His call sign. It is speaking of the very nature, purpose, mission, life and Person of Jesus Christ, the Son of God, the Savior of mankind. To pray "in the name of Jesus" is to align ourselves with the very nature of God, and to abandon ourselves completely to His wisdom and purpose. When we enter that place of communion with God in prayer, our prayer is always answered.

As alluded to earlier, answered prayer comes in different forms. Often we see a direct answer to our prayer. A cancer miraculously disappears. A person is instantly freed from some addiction. A broken relationship is miraculously restored. A financial need is met, seemingly from out of nowhere. Literally billions of direct answers to prayer. Yet sometimes the problem we're seeking help with is not actually our primary problem, but is in fact a symptom of a deeper wound. So we also often see God answer our prayer by bringing healing to that deeper wound, instead of the situation we perceived to be the problem. And often too our problem could be caused by a number of underlying issues, all of which might need to be healed before the problem we're aware of can be resolved. That's why it is so important to prevail in prayer; to not falter or give up. The messes in our lives come from a myriad of sources, often outside us and beyond our control, some even stemming from issues arising early in childhood or even in previous generations of our family. So healing a particular problem can sometimes require extensive prayer, sometimes even years of prayer, to deal with all the underlying issues. But we can trust that God is at work in our prayer, pointing us toward those issues that most need healing, healing them as we bring them before Him, and strengthening and encouraging us on our journey.

And it can even be said that in some cases our suffering benefits us (and others) even more greatly than not suffering would, because it can lead us to utter dependence on God. For it is in that complete surrendering to God that we find our ultimate healing, eternal life with God. I suspect that some suffering is allowed by God simply for that very reason, because although painful at the time, it assists us in our journey toward heaven. In that sense some sufferings can be redemptive in nature. But if our suffering is not offered to God in prayer, united with Christ's suffering on the cross, then it just remains valueless, non-redemptive suffering. It just plain hurts.

That brings us full circle back to those horrific situations we find inexplicable and almost unbearably painful. For example, an innocent child, in spite of the fervent prayer of the parents and the community, dies of leukemia. Where is God in that? Certainly God did not change that course of events in answer to our prayer, and frankly, we'll never know why this side of heaven. In those situations I can only respond as the Apostle Peter did when he too was faced with an inexplicable mystery, turning to Jesus in surrender and asking "Lord, to whom shall we go? You have the words of eternal life" (John 6:68). In the face of heartbreaking loss, truly where else can I turn? As Peter observed, only God offers the ultimate healing of all our pain and suffering—eternal life with Him.

Some of the miracles mentioned in the Bible seem preposterous. For example how could Jonah spend three days underwater in the stomach of a fish, and not suffocate or be digested by the fish?

I don't know. When I get to heaven I'll ask Jonah.

But what if Jonah's not in heaven when you get there?

Then you ask him.

Sorry. Just kidding.

But seriously, consider this: God, though Creator of all that we can see, hear and touch in the physical realm, stands before, after, and apart from the physical. Although He is Author of all the laws of nature, He is subject to none of them. While we understand our world within the context of time, God is timeless, and is subject to no measure of time. We develop precise tools that can measure almost any aspect of the physical realm, yet God can be measured by none of them. In fact, the miracles of God are called miracles for the very reason that they can't be readily explained by any of the known laws of nature. Miracles, big or small, derive from the supernatural power of God. It's unreasonable, therefore to expect miracles to be explainable in terms of the natural.

But I really do hope to see Jonah in heaven. I'd really like to ask him how God kept him alive in that fish for three days. I'm as curious as you are.

On and off through the centuries, Christians in different parts of the world have sometimes killed each other, and killed people from other religions as well. People from other religions have sometimes done the same. Isn't religion the source of many problems in the world?

Having observed mankind's behavior over the past seven decades, I'm convinced that no one kills someone else simply because of theology. People kill each other over pride, power, money, anger, control, jealousy, revenge, and all the other usual reasons. Sometimes however, religion is used as an excuse, or manipulated as a motivator, to incite others to get them to go kill for you. Cortez brings 2000 soldiers and 2 priests to the New World. Is he really there to bring salvation to the pagans? (Perhaps if he had brought 2000 priests and 2 soldiers we could believe that). Is the current war between Shiite and Sunni Muslims really about some affront to Mohammad, or is it about power, control, and oil revenue?

Religion is not the source of the world's problems. But it is periodically misappropriated by some as an excuse to act in very irreligious ways; just as are racial differences, cultural differences, tribal differences, governmental differences, etc.

Evolution to me seems to be an irrefutable fact. Doesn't the theory of evolution disprove the notion of a God?

Not at all. I'll explain why in a moment, but first let me point out where different Christians stand on this question.

On the one hand, some Christians hold to a very literal interpretation of the genealogies discussed in the Bible. From those genealogies they calculate the length of time that mankind has existed to be thousands, not millions, of years. Most of those Christians accept no element of evolutionary theory as fact. Nor do they accept that the earth is billions of years old.

At the other end of the spectrum, some Christians accept virtually every aspect of evolutionary theory as fact, except that they believe God initiated the creation process and continues to direct it along the way. So they still acknowledge God as Creator. If there was a "big bang" that started all this, they believe that God willed and directed it.

Between those two widely divergent views we find Christians who don't question science's methods for measuring the age of the earth, but who absolutely refute the evolutionary theory that all existing species of life "evolved" from earlier species. Regarding time, they note that the Bible states that "With the Lord a day is like a thousand years, and a thousand years are like a day" (2 Peter 3:8), thereby reasoning that one can't calculate God's time by man's units of measure. Thus they conclude that when the Bible says God created something in a "day", it could just as easily mean a billion years.

However, they find the many theories on the origin and evolution of the species to be both unbiblical and unsupportable by physical evidence. In their view, many people are mistakenly confusing the changes observed *within* species through selective breeding, natural selection, or gene mutation with "evolution." For example, if you and I could live many thousands or millions of years, these Christians wouldn't doubt the possibility that you and I could, beginning with a kennel full of Chihuahuas, selectively breed canines until we ended up with dogs the size of elephants. But they contend that neither science, nor the Bible, supports the theory that we (or "nature") could selectively breed Chihuahuas until we *actually had* elephants. They might also point out that while the secular world seems to have simply accepted the theory of evolution as fact, in truth the possibility of the evolution of any one species into a new or different species remains a completely unproven hypothesis.

All of which brings me to the point that the theory of evolution does not test the existence of God at all, except in the imagination of those who want to propose that it does. At most it attempts to explain the diverse nature of life by examining the physical, using elements assembled from the physical as its tools, and then theorizing on the relationships between species within that physical realm. And while the speculation is interesting, it certainly misses any standard of "proof". In any event, the theory of evolution makes no claim of possessing the methodology to measure the spiritual realm, where we find God, the font of all creation.

Nobody can prove to me that God exists. I've even heard some Christians admit that. What do you say to that?!!

I say I'd like to have a word with those Christians.

However, I suppose that if the only type of evidence one is willing to consider is forensic evidence, then perhaps God's existence can't be proven within that restrictive paradigm. After all, God is not of this creation, as discussed under previous topics. You can't expect to find God's DNA on the branches of a burnt bush, or His fingerprints on a stone tablet. But I ask you, is it reasonable to exclude all but forensic evidence when searching for truth? Consider the following analogy:

Fifteen tourists are standing on a sidewalk waiting for their tour bus to pick them up. Startled by two explosively loud pops, they all look across the narrow street in the direction of the disturbance just in time to see me running out the front door of a convenience store carrying a revolver and a bag. They watch me throw the gun and the bag through the open window of a car idling at the curb. But as I open the door to climb in, the driver (my accomplice) spots a police cruiser in his rear view mirror turning the corner onto our street. Panicking, he hits the gas, leaving me abandoned on the sidewalk, staring in stunned disbelief at the fifteen people looking at me from just across the way. Finally coming to my senses, I take off on foot in the direction of my disappearing get-away car. The officers in the cruiser didn't hear the shots, but the driver does catch a glimpse of someone (me) running around the corner at the far end of the block. Then they spot the fifteen tourists waving wildly at them.

As the cruiser approaches, the crowd yells that they heard shots, and that a man with a gun just ran out of the store and down the street. As the driver of the police cruiser accelerates the car in pursuit of me, his partner beside him radios for backup. Within a couple of blocks, the officers corral me. While they are handcuffing me, their backup arrives and enters the convenience store. There they find the store owner dead on the floor with two bullet holes in his chest, an empty, opened cash drawer, and the rear door of the store secured by a deadbolt from the inside.

The police never do find my accomplice, nor do they recover the weapon or the stolen cash. But in a lineup, twelve of the fifteen tourists positively identify me as the one running out of the store with a gun. Two of the fifteen tourists, however, state they can't be sure. And one of the fifteen thinks that the perpetrator was Hispanic, so insists that none of us in the lineup could be the man, as all of us appear to be Anglo.

At my trial, the defense attorney tries to generate doubt by emphasizing the testimony of the lone witness who believes a Hispanic man committed the crime. He also tries to leverage the statement of the two witnesses who said they couldn't be sure, to question whether any of the witnesses could truly be sure. Finally he attacks minor differences in the witnesses' testimony, such as the fact that some of the witnesses thought I was wearing a dark green jersey, while others thought it was blue. But all twelve witnesses hold fast to their testimony that they are absolutely certain it was me running out of that store with the gun.

Unless a grave miscarriage of justice occurs, I will rightfully be convicted of murder, because the acceptable burden of proof under the law is defined as "beyond a reasonable doubt." And although no forensic evidence was recovered, and even though the testimony was not 100% consistent in its details, it was still compelling, and effectively established a reasonable proof of my guilt; which is exactly what the jury concludes. At sentencing I might well be ordered to prison for life.

Now I ask you, if it is reasonable to lock up a person for life based on the sworn testimony of reliable witnesses, isn't it reasonable to consider sworn testimony in the question of whether God exists?

So let me just quickly summarize the testimonial evidence available to us:

First we have the testimony of Jesus' proclamations, in which He testified that He was the Son of God, One in Being with God the Father, the one Mediator between God and Man, the I Am, the Alpha and the Omega, the Beginning and the End, the Author of Life, the only path to eternal life.

Next we have the testimony of Jesus' miracles: healing the sick, restoring sight to the blind, casting out demons, walking on water, multiplying the loaves, turning water into wine, raising the dead, and on and on, witnessed by thousands of His contemporaries.

Then we have the testimony of Jesus' resurrection. Scourged to the edge of death, spiked to a cross and hung until dead; then even run through by a Roman soldier's spear. All of this very public and witnessed by many hundreds of onlookers. Then three days later rising from the dead, appearing first before dozens of witnesses, then hundreds, finally ascending into heaven right before the eyes of His disciples.

Then of course we have the testimony, some of it written and preserved even to this day, of His disciples. Not only did they testify to the statements Jesus made and to the miracles that Jesus performed, but empowered by the Holy Spirit, they continued to perform similar miracles themselves, even restoring life to the dead.

But lest any of us speculate that perhaps the disciples just found preaching a better gig than commercial fishing or tent making (maybe even embellishing their testimony a bit to fatten the collection plate) we have the testimony of their martyrdom. When pressed, under penalty of death, to withdraw their testimony concerning Jesus, they chose death. Under no circumstances would they deny the Author of Life, because they *knew* what they had witnessed with their own eyes and they *knew* who Jesus was. And *they* knew God would restore them to eternal life, because Jesus had proven that His promises were trustworthy.

Not only do we have the testimony of the martyrdom of the first disciples, but we also have the testimony of countless thousands of later martyrs who also willingly surrendered their lives rather than denounce the Savior they'd come to know experientially, personally, and undeniably.

Then there's the testimony of billions of other Christians throughout the centuries, including countless volumes written by many of them attesting to their tangible, unmistakable encounters with God through the risen Christ.

But perhaps some would disqualify the testimony of all the aforementioned Christians based on the claim that those witnesses are no longer alive and thus can't be cross examined. Yet even were we to disqualify that evidence, we still have the testimony of a couple billion other Christians still alive today, residing all over the globe, as well as access to untold thousands of books written by these contemporaries testifying to their personal experience of God.

And finally, if we're just not willing to accept any evidence other than our own firsthand witness; then we need simply invite Jesus Christ into our lives. Surrender our lives to Him and ask Him to reveal Himself to us. Join a church and a Bible study. Seek Him with sincerity and openness. He will show up I promise! Then one day we can write our own testimony, just as I've done here.

Final Appeal

My friend, I do not believe that it is by chance that you are reading this testimony, but that you have been called to this testimony through the intentional intercession of God. I believe God is speaking to you this very moment through His Son, Jesus Christ. *Today* is your day. I pray that you will say "yes" to Jesus and open your heart to Him. I assure you that if you invite Jesus into your life, He will not fail to enter in and bring new life and joy and freedom, and a peace that surpasses all understanding. He is calling you now...

"Here I am. I stand at the door and knock. If anyone hears my voice and opens the door, I will come in and eat with him, and he with me. To him who overcomes, I will give the right to sit with me on my throne, just as I overcame and sat down with my Father on his throne."

REVELATION 3:20-21

"For God so loved the world that he gave his
one and only Son, that whoever believes in
him shall not perish but have eternal life."

JOHN 3:15

Glory be to the Father, and to the Son, and to the Holy Spirit!

Bill Odell
Ellensburg, Washington
March 18, 2020

About
A Witness to Christ Ministries

A Witness to Christ Ministries was founded by the author of this book to advance the following goals:

- To provide compelling testimony to non-Christians of the reality of Jesus Christ, the Son of God; His person, life, mission, and glorious promise of eternal life in heaven to all who would accept and follow Him.

- To provide non-Christians a vision of the reality that they too can personally confirm the existence of God.

- To provide a road map and an invitation to non-Christians for entering into a personal encounter with Jesus Christ, the Author of life and Savior to a broken world.

- To provide fellow Christians with tools to help them effectively profess Christ to non-believing friends and family members.

- To provide encouragement to fellow Christians, and to offer suggestions and resources for deepening their own personal experience of God.

- To promote dialogue between the churches, and continued reconciliation within the Body of Christ.

For questions, comments or for information on bulk order pricing, please contact the author at:

A.WitnesstoChrist@comcast.net
